Uniforms & Equipment of the French Armed Forces in World War I

Uniforms & Equipment of the French Armed Forces in World War I

Spencer A. Coil

Schiffer Military History
Atglen, PA

ACKNOWLEDGMENTS

First and foremost, I would like to acknowledge and dedicate this work to all those who served in the Great War, especially those who appear in these photographs, and above all to my family, who supported and stood by me every step of the way, especially my ***Mother***, ***Aunt Frankie***, and ***Grandmother***!

I would like to thank the following individuals who directly or indirectly assisted in the creation of this work:

Frédéric Gouraud (expert, specialist, enthusiast, historian)
Steve Smith Studios (professional photographers Tel; 1 636 343 7606)
The Ezzo Family, especially Dipl. Ing. Blahad Ezzo (experts and enthusiasts)
The Pomeranzeva-Halikin Family (historians, experts, enthusiasts, and linguists)
The Hornkohl Family (enthusiasts)
The Otte Family (enthusiasts)
Frau Dr. Grafin Irene Montjoye and her son, Herr Mag. Graf Douglas Montjoye (authors, journalists, enthusiasts, historians)
Dan Eibeck (historian, expert, specialist, enthusiast, archaeologist, curator)
Mag. Clemens Ellmauthaler (historian, expert, specialist, enthusiast, author)
Fulvio Rizzo (historian, expert, specialist, enthusiast)
Professor Dr. Renato Zavattini and family (historians, experts, specialists, enthusiasts)
Professor Del Schwinke
President Dr. David Harpool
President Dr. Wil Goodheer
Vice President Dr. L. Boyer
Alexei Grichine (expert, specialist, historian)
Salvatore Vasta

My Students, especially those from Croatia who informed me of the origin of the necktie in the French Army.

A special thanks to internationally acclaimed and recognized military medals and decorations experts, specialists, and enthusiasts Herr und Frau Mag. Hartmut und Christine Rochowanski, who have maintained an impeccable reputation for over 30 years, and Franz Zabernig and family. Finally, thanks to the Schiffer team for all of the outstanding work all of you have done! The books just keep getting better!

Book design by Ian Robertson.

Library of Congress Control Number: 2005929231

Printed in China.
ISBN: 0-7643-2269-9

We are interested in hearing from authors with book ideas on related topics.

Published by Schiffer Publishing Ltd.
4880 Lower Valley Road
Atglen, PA 19310
Phone: (610) 593-1777
FAX: (610) 593-2002
E-mail: Info@schifferbooks.com.
Visit our web site at: www.schifferbooks.com
Please write for a free catalog.
This book may be purchased from the publisher.
Please include $3.95 postage.
Try your bookstore first.

In Europe, Schiffer books are distributed by:
Bushwood Books
6 Marksbury Avenue
Kew Gardens
Surrey TW9 4JF
England
Phone: 44 (0) 20 8392-8585
FAX: 44 (0) 20 8392-9876
E-mail: Info@bushwoodbooks.co.uk.
Free postage in the UK. Europe: air mail at cost.
Try your bookstore first.

Contents

Introduction

Various headdresses, uniforms, and equipment were used by *poilus* (French soldiers) during the First World War. Older models and newer models of headdresses, uniforms, and equipment were often combined, giving *poilus* an eclectic and varied appearance in the trenches and on the battlefield. A *poilu* could enhance his appearance and outfit by combining issued, privately purchased, and homemade headdresses, uniforms, and equipment as well.

Headdress

The *kepi* (field cap) was a popular headdress with soldiers of all ranks, and was worn throughout the First World War. *Kepis* varied in shape and size, and were made from various cloths. A *kepi* could be stiffened or given a crushed look. Officers and NCOs preferred a stiffened style, while enlisted ranks fashioned a crushed or relaxed style of *kepi*. Most *kepis* were made from various grades of wool; however, other materials were also used, such as velvet. *Kepis* ranged in color and combinations of colors from black, red, and dark blue to horizon blue (*bleu horizon*). The Foreign Legion preferred wearing white cloth covers over their *kepis*, which often had a piece of cloth to cover the back of the soldier's neck. The white kepi, often referred to as *kepi blanc*, was a symbol of a Legionnaire. Ornate piping could be stitched to the exterior of a *kepi*, which often indicated rank and branch of service. Also, rank or branch of service could be indicated on the front of the *kepi* just above the visor, or on the two buttons that secured the chinstrap. The interior of a *kepi* was often lined with cotton or silk, and had a leather sweatband stitched to it. The visors on *kepis* were made of leather or a composite material. Many visors can be found with fine cracks, depending upon age and exposure to the elements. The *kepi* itself offered very little protection to a soldier's head, therefore, most soldiers wore metal skullcaps underneath their *kepi* while in the trenches or on the battlefield.

Another style of cloth headdress was the *calot*, or *bonnet de police*, as it was sometimes called, which was a tent shaped forage cap; it was often made from various materials, such as corduroy, but most commonly was made of wool. Often a *calotte* had regimental numbers or distinctions fastened or stitched on, in addition to various colored piping that denoted rank or branch of service. Normally, rank and branch of service distinctions were located at the front or on the sides of a *calotte*.

Berets were preferred by many *poilus* and came in various shapes and sizes. Oversized berets were worn for the large part in the pre to early war years; however, as the war progressed, the berets shrunk in size and became more fitted. Most berets were made of wool and came in various colors, but the majority were either black, dark blue, or *bleu horizon*. Rank or branch of service insignia were either stitched or fastened to the front of the beret, however, many berets bore no insignia at all. Some berets were lined, but the majority were not. When worn by a *chasseur* this headdress was called a *tarte*. Organized in battalions, *chasseurs*—which translates as "hunters"—were the riflemen, skirmishers, scouts, and sharpshooters of the French Armed forces, and had many nuances in their vocabulary and mannerisms. Examples of such nuances in their vocabulary are seen in the terms used for distinguishing colors, such as "*jonquille*" (canary) for the color yellow, and "*bleu cherise*" (cherry blue) for the color red. *Chasseur* mannerisms were influenced by their beliefs. For example, a *chasseur* does not live in "*une caserne*," or barracks; rather, in "*un quartier*" (quarter), and they bleed a different color blood on the battlefield. Their nuances aside, they distinguished themselves on the battlefield with their cunning and bravery. Their German foe regarded the chasseurs as "*Die blauen Teufel*," or the blue devils, because of their tenacity on the battlefield and their attitude of never wanting to be captured alive. *Les Diables Bleus*, as the blue devils were called in French, were legendary for their valor, as well.

Colonials, Zouaves, and Tirailleurs wore a *chéchia*, which was a cylindrical wool cap with a tassel fastened on top. Normally, a *chéchia* was made of red wool and had a moon and star motif insignia stitched or fastened to the front. Other regiment or unit distinctions were either stitched or fastened on, and many a *chéchia* bore no distinctions at all. Other indigenous troops, such as the Annamese, wore woven bamboo hats that were conical in shape and covered with cloth.

The official arrival of the Adrian steel helmet in 1915 (*Modele 1915 Casque Adrian*) did not eliminate cloth headdress from being worn in the trenches and on the battlefield. Its arrival did, however, cause the cloth headdress to be allocated to a role as a supplement to a soldier's headdress, rather than being the only means of protecting his head. Adrian steel helmets were manufactured under first French patent (*Brevet*), and later exported to France's colonies and other allied nations, such as Russia and Italy. Russia and Italy manufactured various other models based on the *Casque Adrian*. The inspiration for the design of the *Casque Adrian* can be seen in the helmets worn by French firemen.

The two parallel openings located on the front of the *Casque Adrian* allowed a die stamped unit identification badge to be fastened on like a brad. There were badges for various branches of service, such as infantry, artillery, administration, medical, marine infantry, chasseurs, engineers, Zouaves, and Tirailleurs. The letters "RF" (*République Français*) appear on most badges. *Casque Adrian* liners were leather, and often corrugated metal strips were placed between the liner and the helmet. The helmet's chinstrap, or *jugulaire*, was made of leather, and was held in place by the visor when not in use. Chinstraps were either crafted as flat or braided leather strips. Helmets were painted in various shades of blue gray. Earlier models were painted a darker shade of blue gray and had a gloss finish, while later models were a lighter shade of blue with a matte finish. Cloth helmet covers were also available, and were often used to help camouflage the helmet. When the *l' artillerie spéciale* (tanks) arrived on the battlefield later in the war, tank crewmembers modified their helmets by removing the front visor, which allowed them to have more maneuverability and visibility inside the tank.

Marine infantry serving in the colonies, as well as those in the Dardanelles and later Macedonia, wore cloth-covered pith helmets with or without metal unit badges, in addition to their sailor caps with a pom-pom on top. Other branches of service, depending upon availability and need, wore pith helmets as well. Pith helmets were made of either cork or leather, and had a vent located at the top.

At the outbreak of the war, the cavalry was outfitted in headdress reminiscent of that worn by the French cavalry in the Franco-Prussian War, and the post war years that followed. The cavalry wore both shakos—which were normally leather or wool—and plumed helmets, which were either shiny steel or brass. Adaptations and modifications were made to the ornately crafted shiny brass and steel headdresses, such as covering them with cloth; however, it proved nevertheless to be too decadent and cumbersome for the battlefield, and therefore it became obsolete.

An aviator (*aviateur*) preferred a durable, light weight headdress made of leather, because it offered the most protection from the elements. When leather headdress was not available or not needed cloth headdress was used. In addition to having issued headdress, aviators also purchased them from private manufacturers. The leather flight helmets were covered with oil cloth and/or treated canvas-like material, and most were stamped or embossed with the word "*Brevet*" (Patent). The flight helmet most often associated with aviators from the First World War was known as a Roold. An aviator could also purchase other headdress related accoutrements from private manufacturers, such as goggles (*les lunettes*).

It is important to take into consideration that a variety of dyes, paints, and materials were used in making headdress, and therefore colors and overall appearance vary from piece to piece. It is also important to consider the variations in color and appearance caused by exposure to the elements, particularly sunlight. These factors should not only be considered for headdress, but for uniforms and equipment, as well.

Uniforms

Throughout the course of the war, *poilus* wore certain uniform accoutrements that enhanced their appearance and reflected centuries old French military tradition. One of the many examples of accoutrements can be seen in photos of *poilus* wearing neckties, or *cravates*.

Owing its origin to Croatia and to the Croatian soldiers who fought in the Thirty Years War (1618-48), the necktie has been a part of the French army since the time of Louis XIV. The etymology of the French word for necktie, or *cravate*, is found in the phrase "*a la Croate*," or "*as a Croat*," thus attributing it to the style of Croatian born soldiers who served in French Hussar Regiments.

In addition to *la cravate*, many soldiers chose to wear starched cotton neck guards on the collars of their tunics to prevent the wool from rubbing against their necks. The cotton collars fastened on smooth, small brass studs or hooks, or buttoned onto celluloid or wood buttons.

Early War

Early in the war many *poilus* would have been outfitted in a dark colored wool waistcoat, or *ras-le-cul*, and madder red trousers, or *les pantalons garance*, or in other clothing reflecting the style of the French soldier in the 19th century.

A *Ras-le-cul* was a waistcoat/tunic with a standing collar and exterior buttons. Normally, these waistcoats/tunics were dark blue or black wool, and had a cotton lining with issue stamps. The buttons on the waistcoat were usually made of brass, and bore a unit motif on the forward side of the button and a manufacturer's name on the reverse. Rank and unit distinctions were stitched to the lower part of the sleeves, or near the collar edges during active service. For maneuvers, rank and unit distinctions were drawn on with chalk, which showed up very well against the dark wool.

Les pantalons garance were the French red trousers dyed with a dye made from the root of an herb native to Eurasia known as madder (*rubia tinctorum*). Later an alizarin dye prepared from madder was used to dye *les pantalons garance*. *Les pantalons garance* were issued with ink issue stamps on the cotton waistband or pockets, or privately tailored. *Les pantalons garance* symbolized the French soldier; however, they were impractical for the battlefields in the First World War, and were therefore gradually replaced with either brown corduroy or horizon blue wool trousers.

Generals and high-ranking officers preferred a dark wool tunic with braids running the length of the chest known as a *dolman*. Usually, there were braids with intricately crafted fasteners spanning the chest. In addition, there was detailed stitching on the collar and sleeves of a *dolman*.

Early war troops, such as the Zouaves and Tirailleurs from the colonies, would have been outfitted differently than those of metropolitan France.

Zouaves

Originally formed in 1830 with Kabyles from the Zouaoua tribe in the Jurjura mountains in Algeria, the first two Zouave battalions were commanded by French officers. The Zouave battalions eventually grew and were made up entirely of Frenchmen, but they still maintained the same North African style of uniform as was worn by the Kabyles, with subtle variations occurring over the course of time.

A Zouave *shama*, or jacket, was made of blue wool and embellished with madder red wool designs. Underneath the *shama* was a vest known as the *sédria*, which was also dark blue wool with madder red wool designs. The *sarouel* were the baggy trousers made of red wool that had a slit located near the front known as a "*Lamoriciére*," which allowed water to be drained after having waded through a stream or lake.

The Arrival of the Model 1915 Horizon Blue Tunic

The Model 1915 horizon blue tunic (*veste/tunique/vareuse modele 1915 bleu horizon*) was subject to various personal interpretations once issued or privately purchased by a *poilu*. Issued tunics were made of various grades of horizon wool, depending upon the supply depot and the overall availability of material. The interior of the tunic was lined with white cotton, and sometimes the sleeves were lined with other materials with various patterns, such as stripes. Other tunics were only partially lined, and the ink issue stamps containing the regiment and date were located on the white cotton lining, as were those issue stamps on the fully lined tunics. The cut of an issued tunic was basic and functional, consisting of two side pockets, buttons that were sometimes exposed, sometimes concealed, and a standing collar. The cuts of the pocket flaps, as well as the size of the pockets, varied. Most pockets on issued tunics had interior pockets and often no button flaps. Buttons were made of metal, and often bore a unit motif, such as a flaming grenade for infantry or crossed cannons for artillery. Maker marks appeared on the back of the buttons with motifs, as well as those which bore no motif at all. Many soldiers purchased wood or celluloid buttons and used them instead. Standing collars varied in height, and unit distinctions, such as regiment numbers, could be sewn or fastened on. Following regimental numbers were two angled strips of cloth running parallel to each other that were known as *soustaches*.

Privately tailored horizon blue tunics were normally worn by officers and NCOs, and varied in materials and cuts. Most were made of wool and sometimes corduroy, particularly those worn by the men serving in the metropolitan army; however, the tunics of those serving in the colonies were made of a heavy khaki cotton. The cut of the tunic consisted of pleated double breast and side pockets, and often a standing or stand-fall collar. While most models and variations of this tunic belted with a single or double pronged leather waist belt, or *ceinturon*, there were others that belted with a cloth waist belt using buttons.

Medals, Rank, and Branch of Service Distinctions

Medals (*medailles*), such as the War Cross, or *Croix de Guerre*, were worn on the upper left breast of a soldier's tunic. Either the entire bronze medal with cloth ribbon (usually silk) was worn, or simply a ribbon bar, which may or may not have had any distinction fastened to it. Other commonly awarded *medailles* were the French Military Medal (*Medaille Militaire*), awarded to NCOs as well as enlisted rank soldiers, and the Legion of Honor medal (*Legion d' Honor*), awarded to both military personnel and civilians. All of the aforementioned medals were worn by *poilus* in the field as well as on parade, or while posing for cabinet portraits.

Rank and branch of service distinctions were worn on the sleeves of a soldier's tunic. Rank distinctions, such as two stitched parallel lines (e.g. // or = for either *Maréchal de Logis-Chef* or *corporal* or *lieutenant*) were stitched just above the cuff of the tunic, while branch of service distinctions were stitched or fastened to the upper arm of the tunic, such as *les chasseur alpins* (elite alpinists), *les ingénieurs* (engineers), or *les grenadiers* (grenade men). A hunting horn, which was a marksmen distinction, was also stitched on the upper part of the sleeve.

Footwear

There were various styles of footwear worn by the French armed forces. Most poilus wore some style of field boot, or *brodequins*. There were various models issued, such as the models 1893, 1912, and 1916. These were laced, hob-nailed, leather ankle boots, the upper parts of which were often reinforced with rivets, particularly the 1912 and 16 models.

In addition to his *brodequins*, a *poilu* would wear cloth puttees, or *molletières*, as well as various styles privately purchased and issued leather leggings. The leggings worn by Zouaves were often referred to as *jambiéres*.

Officers and NCOs preferred wearing cap toed laced leather riding boots, or riding boots that pulled on using canvas or leather pulls located on the inside of the upper part of the boots. These styles of boots were preferred by those serving in the cavalry and air service branches.

Repairs and modifications were made to footwear as needed; for example, replacing leather hob-nailed soles for wooden soles. Wooden hob-nailed soles faired better for those soldiers who had to stand in a damp area for an extended time, such as a sentry.

Equipment

The shapes and styles of equipment used by *poilus* were very distinctive in appearance, and could often be seen being used by soldiers of other allied countries, as well as being put to use after having been captured by those serving in the ranks of the Central Powers armed force.

Poilus carried a distinctively crafted Model 1877 canteen (*Modele 1877 bidon*), often referred to as a *bidon* or *gourde*, which was made of metal, and was either painted or covered with cloth. The canteen had two openings and held approximately one liter of water. Various types of plugs, such as corks, were used to seal the canteen, as were various materials used for the carrying strap, such as woven cloth or leather. A soldier would often attach a regulation metal or enameled drinking cup (*quart réglementaire*) to his *gourde* with either a string or a piece of leather. Troops from the colonies were issued *bidons* of a different shape and design.

Every *poilu* usually carried a *musette*, or bread-bag. The *musette* was used not only to carry rations and/or eating utensils, but other useful items, such as grenades, and therefore would be better described as a general purpose bag. A *musette* was made from various materials, such as canvas or heavy cotton, and its construction was simply a bag with a flap that buttoned over and was suspended by a woven cloth strap that a soldier could simply throw over his shoulder.

The Model 1852 mess kit, or *Modele 1852 gamelle*, was round with a lid on a chain approximately 6 inches (15cm) in length attached to its handles, and the handles were on the side of the mess kit. The *(la) gamelle* was slightly tapered, made of tin coated metal and approximately 4 inches (10cm) deep, and 6 inches (15cm) across the top in diameter.

To secure their equipment, *poilus* had access to a variety of leather straps, or *courroies*, which were usually made from brown or black leather. The longest strap was approximately 67 inches (170cm) long, and was used to secure mess equipment. Normally, there was one of these load bearing straps, or *courroie de charge*, issued per squad. The next size strap was approximately 30 inches (75cm) long, and was used to secure a blanket, tent, or overcoat. Shorter straps, such as side straps (*courroie de cote*), measured approximately 20 inches (50 cm), and were used for strapping an extra pair of *brodequins* (field boots), or another necessary equipment item to the haversack.

The model 1893 haversack, or *Modele 1893 havresac*, was nicknamed the ace of diamonds (*as de carreau*) because of its shape and design. Haversacks were made of various colored canvas, such as black, tan, or grayish green. The canvas covered a wood frame pack with leather straps. Other accoutrements necessary for a soldier's survival, such as a gasmask, were usually carried outside the pack.

Poilus used a variety of gasmasks, or *masques á gaz*, such as the *le M2*, *le tampon*, and *le masque ARS17/18*. *Le M2* was a flexible one piece mask that covered the soldier's entire face. A piece of material in the mask acted as a filter. *Le M2* was first issued to the soldiers in a bag, and later in a rectangular metal container that was painted either *bleu horizon* or khaki. *Le tampon* was constructed from multiple pieces, and filtered out poison gas with a gauze bandage or cloth soaked in a chemical solution, such as hydro cyanic acid, which counteracted phosgene or mustard gas. The ARS17/18, whose designation stood for *Appareil Respiratoire Spécial 1917/18*, was constructed from multiple pieces, and was carried in a cylindrical metal canister with either a fluted or smooth design. It had a leather, string, or woven cloth carrying strap. Other models of *masques á gaz* were also worn by *poilus*, such as those obtained from other allies, or those captured from the central powers.

Equipment For A Squad (*Une Escouade*)

There were other items that were issued to poilus in limited quantities, such as mess or cooking equipment. One such item was the Model 1886 coffee mill/grinder, or *Modele 1886 Moulin à Café*, which was a hand cranked grinder with a removable handle that could be stored for easy transportation. Large marmite pots, or *marmite de bouthéon*, held cooked food portions for roughly a squad of men, just as the large metal plate with canvas cover (*plat à quatre*) was intended for similar use. It is also interesting to note that civilian French kitchen cutlery, or *coutelier*, also saw use in the trenches and on the battlefield for other purposes than serving the culinary needs of *une escouade*. Trench knifes used by *poilus* were often modified kitchen knives, and proved to be very useful for multiple purposes, as well as demonstrating the ingenuity of the hardy and resourceful French soldiers.

Another item issued in limited quantities was the Model 1881 collapsible water bucket, or *Modele 1881 Seau en Toile*. The water bucket was made of waterproof canvas, and was very useful for carrying water, or when flooding occurred in the trenches. The Model 1910 collapsible lantern (*Modele Lanterne à Bougie*) was also issued in limited quantities. The lantern was three-sided, with a candle holder inside, and was made of tin coated metal and celluloid or glass.

Tools were items crucial to a *poilus'* survival, such as shovels, wire cutters, single or doubled pointed picks, and saws. Shovels, which were issued in limited quantities, included the model 1879 shovel (*modele 1879 pelle portative*), the larger model, and the model 1916 shovel (*modele 1916 pelle ronde portative*), the smaller model. Two models of issued wire cutters included the *modele 1905 petite cisaill*, the smaller model, and the *modele 1888 grande cisaille*, the larger model. The two models of picks issued were the model 1909 single pointed pick, or *modele 1909 pelle pioche*, and the model 1916 double pointed pick, or *modele 1916 pioche portative*. The saw issued was the model 1879 saw (*modele 1879 scie articulée*).

In addition to most of the aforementioned issued equipment, much civilian or privately made equipment was used as well by the French armed forces in the First World War. Civilian or privately made equipment was often preferred over issued by *poilus* for either functional or sentimental value, and regulations did not rigidly address or forbid its use or presence, since a soldier's trench or dugout was his home. The presence of civilian amenities, be it functional or sentimental, often had positive effects on the morale of a soldier in an army evolving to meet the demands of internal and external conflicts, such as mutiny and mechanized warfare.

Observations on Nuances in the French Armed Forces

The array of materials available for production of uniforms and equipment for French troops was vast, drawing not only on domestic resources, but also on what could be obtained from the colonies, as well as imports from the allied countries during the Great War. In addition, production and usage of uniforms and equipment was effected by social, political, and economic conditions in France during this period.

The French armed forces, as all the other armed forces of the participating nations during the Great War, were forced to evolve and make developments in their uniforms and equipment. Industry could not readily respond to this forced evolution and development that was needed during the war and the years that followed after the war to end all wars. Industrial complexes, particularly military, rose to meet the demands and needs of a market. Yet there was only so much that could be done to meet these demands. Due to this fact, there are chapters covering pre to early war and late to post war uniforms and equipment that will show that the armed forces used what was available during and after the war. The introduction of horizon blue uniforms and Adrian helmets in 1915 were innovations that addressed, but did not entirely meet, the demands and needs of the armed forces. In the years following, the armies of occupation faced the same outfitting needs and demands. Therefore, the armed forces in the years following very much resembled the armed forces during the war.

The black and white period photos, as well as the photos of original uniforms and equipment in the color gallery, will enable people to visualize the *poilus* and their plights during the Great War, or *la Premiere Guerre*. In many ways this work will pose more questions than answers, and that is precisely its purpose. Period photos, as well as period objects, are the only source available when trying to accurately visualize an era in history. Beyond period photos, the only options left for visualization are archeological finds, as well as artistic and author renditions. When looking at this collection of photos, questions should be asked beyond the answers given in the captions, and personal interpretations are encouraged, as this work is meant to have application.

History, like collecting, is a journey that does not always have a destination. Journeying through these pages of photos should be enjoyable, as well as informative. In addition to remembering all those in the photos who served, it is important to remember that each of these photos takes the place of a thousand words.

Chapter One

Machineguns

Three *chasseurs* preparing to fire a French-manufactured Hotchkiss 8mm caliber machinegun, or *la mitrailleuse Hotchkiss*. The metal magazine strip held a maximum of 30 rounds. These men are identified as *chasseurs* because of the hunting horn motif that appears on their steel Model 1915 Adrian helmets (*Modele 1915 Casques Adrian*) and below the cloth numbers on their overcoat collar insignia. In addition, all carry 8mm caliber French-manufactured Lebel bolt-action rifles with magazines holding up to eight rounds.

Four *poilus* from the *36e Régiment* manning a M1907 8mm caliber St. Etienne machinegun. The St. Etienne machinegun was designed by the French government and manufactured at the St. Etienne Arsenal. The *poilu* preparing to feed the 30 round metal magazine strip wears a privately tailored corduroy uniform.

This group of *poilus* display the various models of machineguns used by the French armed forces during the First World War. In addition to the 8mm caliber, French-manufactured Hotchkiss and St. Etienne, is an Imperial German manufactured Maxim (*Machinengewehr 08*), which was most likely captured during a raid.

The soldiers on the right are manning a captured Imperial German manufactured Maxim (*Machinengewehr 08*), and the soldiers on the left man an 8mm caliber, French-manufactured Model 1905 Puteaux, or *modele 1905 mitrailleuse Puteaux*.

These four *poilus* are manning an 8mm French-manufactured Hotchkiss machinegun, or *la mitrailleuse Hotchkiss*. In addition, they are armed with 8mm, French-manufactured Lebel rifles, wear steel Model 1915 Adrian helmets (*Modele 1915 Casques Adrian*) with infantry insignia, and are from the *156e Régiment*, as the collar patch insignia (*pattes de collet de troupes*) on their overcoats indicates.

The soldiers in this group are armed with 8mm, French-manufactured Lebel rifles and Hotchkiss machineguns.

These soldiers are armed with a 8mm Hotchkiss machinegun (*la mitrailleuse Hotchkiss*) and a French light machinegun known as a *Chauchat*.

This group of *poilus* are from the 113e *Régiment*, as the numbers on their kepis and collars indicate. They are manning an 8mm Hotchkiss machinegun, or *la mitrailleuse Hotchkiss*. In addition, the mustached soldier standing on the right is holding a piece of observation equipment with leather carrying strap. On the reverse of this photo is *"8e Section des Mitrailleusse, 18 Décembre 1915."*

This group of *poilus* are posed behind an 8mm Hotchkiss machinegun, or *la mitrailleuse Hotchkiss*. The Hotchkiss was designed by Benjamin Berkeley Hotchkiss, who was born in Watertown, Connecticut, in 1826, and founded the Hotchkiss Company, located at Route de Gonesse in Saint-Denis, France, in 1867.

Most *poilus* in this group are clad in wool *calottes*, or forage caps, and Model 1915 horizon-blue tunics, or *Veste Modele 1915 bleu horizon*. They appear ready for action with their 8mm Lebel rifle and Hotchkiss machinegun.

These seven mustached men are from the *42e Régiment*, as the numbers on kepis and collars indicate. Mounted on tripods are an observation piece (left), Hotchkiss 8mm caliber machinegun (center), and a M1907 8mm caliber St. Etienne machinegun (right).

This group of *poilus* man a M1907 8mm caliber St. Etienne machinegun and wear a variety of kepis, tunics (*vareuses*), and overcoats. This photo is dated May 9, 1915.

These *poilus* are from the 206e *Régiment*, as the cloth numbers on the collars of their overcoats indicate. They are armed with 8mm caliber Lebel rifles and Model 1907 St. Etienne machineguns. This photo is dated December 1915.

This group of *poilus* proudly pose with their 8mm caliber Model 1907 St. Etienne machinegun. The cloth numbers on the collars of their Model 1915 horizon blue tunics indicate their unit. The soldier standing on the right has been awarded the War Cross, or *Croix de Guerre*.

A group of *poilus* from the 129e and 329e *Régiments*, clad in various models of tunics, pose with their 8mm caliber Model 1907 St. Etienne machinegun in this 1915 vintage photo.

Three *poilus* wearing Model 1915 horizon blue tunics and helmets with artillery badges pose for a photo outside of their tent with a 8mm caliber Model 1907 St. Etienne machinegun. Their collars bear no regimental numbers, and their tunics are belted with either single or double-pronged leather belts.

Four *poilus* wearing Model 1915 horizon blue tunics and helmets feed strips holding 30 8mm caliber rounds into their Model 1907 St. Etienne machinegun. The two boxes on the ground are for transporting ammunition. This photo is dated March 13, 1917.

Ten *poilus* pose for a photo with their 8mm caliber Model 1907 St. Etienne machinegun. The date on the reverse side of this photo is May 9, 1915.

Near a stone cottage with slate roof in the French countryside, 12 *poilus* wearing various models of kepis, tunics, and overcoats pose for a photo on a dirt road with their 8mm caliber Model 1907 St. Etienne machinegun. The soldier in the dark colored wool tunic has the number "27" on his dark colored wool kepi. May 16, 1915.

This group of *poilus* proudly poses with their two 8mm caliber Model 1907 St. Etienne machineguns. Some of them have been awarded the War Cross, or *Croix de Guerre*.

In a wooded area near the front, a company of *poilus* clad in various models of kepis and overcoats pose for a photo with their 8mm caliber Model 1907 St. Etienne machinegun.

This group of *poilus*, clad in various styles of tunics and fatigues, poses with their observation equipment and 8mm caliber Model 1907 St. Etienne machinegun. In addition, the soldier wearing the dark wool tunic has a marksman badge stitched to his left sleeve.

Clad in various models of forage caps, kepis, and tunics, this group of *poilus* poses proudly with their two 8mm caliber Model 1907 St. Etienne machineguns. The reverse side of this photo is dated 1917.

This group of *poilus*, posing with their two 8mm caliber Hotchkiss machineguns, is from the 152e *Régiment*, as the numbers on their collars indicate.

These *poilus* dressed in Model 1915 tunics pose proudly with their 8mm caliber Model 1907 St. Etiennes and Hotchkiss machineguns.

This was commercially produced during the First World War, depicting an 8mm Hotchkiss machinegun section.

This was commercially produced during the First World War, depicting an 8mm caliber Model 1907 St. Etienne machinegun section preparing for combat.

The second squad from the 21st Dragoon Regiment proudly display their two Chauchats.

This group of *poilus*, wearing fatigues and forage caps, is armed with Chauchat light machineguns and Lebel rifles.

These *poilus* are from the 156e *Régiment* and are armed with Lebel rifles and a Chauchat light machine gun.

These *poilus* are from the 156e *Régiment* and are armed with Lebel rifles and a Chauchat light machine gun.

These *poilus* wear Model 1915 Adrian helmets with canvas covers, and horizon blue wool tunics with the numbers "403" stitched to their collars. They pose for this photo with an 8mm caliber Model 1907 St. Etienne machinegun mounted on a tripod.

Four *poilus* manning an 8mm caliber Model 1907 St. Etienne machinegun mounted on a tripod with two wheels.

Chapter Two

Medical

Sisters, nurses, priests, surgeons, and patients pose for a group photo outside of a grotto, France 1915.

Tirailleurs, *chasseurs*, and other *poilus*. Southern France 1917.

Some of the first casualties of the war pose for a group photo with their nurses. Many, if not all, would soon be returning to the trenches. Lyon 1914.

Nurses, *Marine d' Infanterie*, and other *poilus*, 1916.

These *poilus* were some of the first casualties of the war. 1914.

Poilus humor, France 1917.

A group of nurses, medics, and soldiers from other branches of service pose for a group photo on the hospital grounds. June 8, 1915.

Among the other *poilus* in this group photo are *poilu* from the 153e, 220e, 195e, 120e, and 34e Regiments. The *poilu* from the 220e Regiment standing on the far left has cloth sapper insignia stitched to both sleeves of his overcoat, and two war service chevrons stitched to his left sleeve.

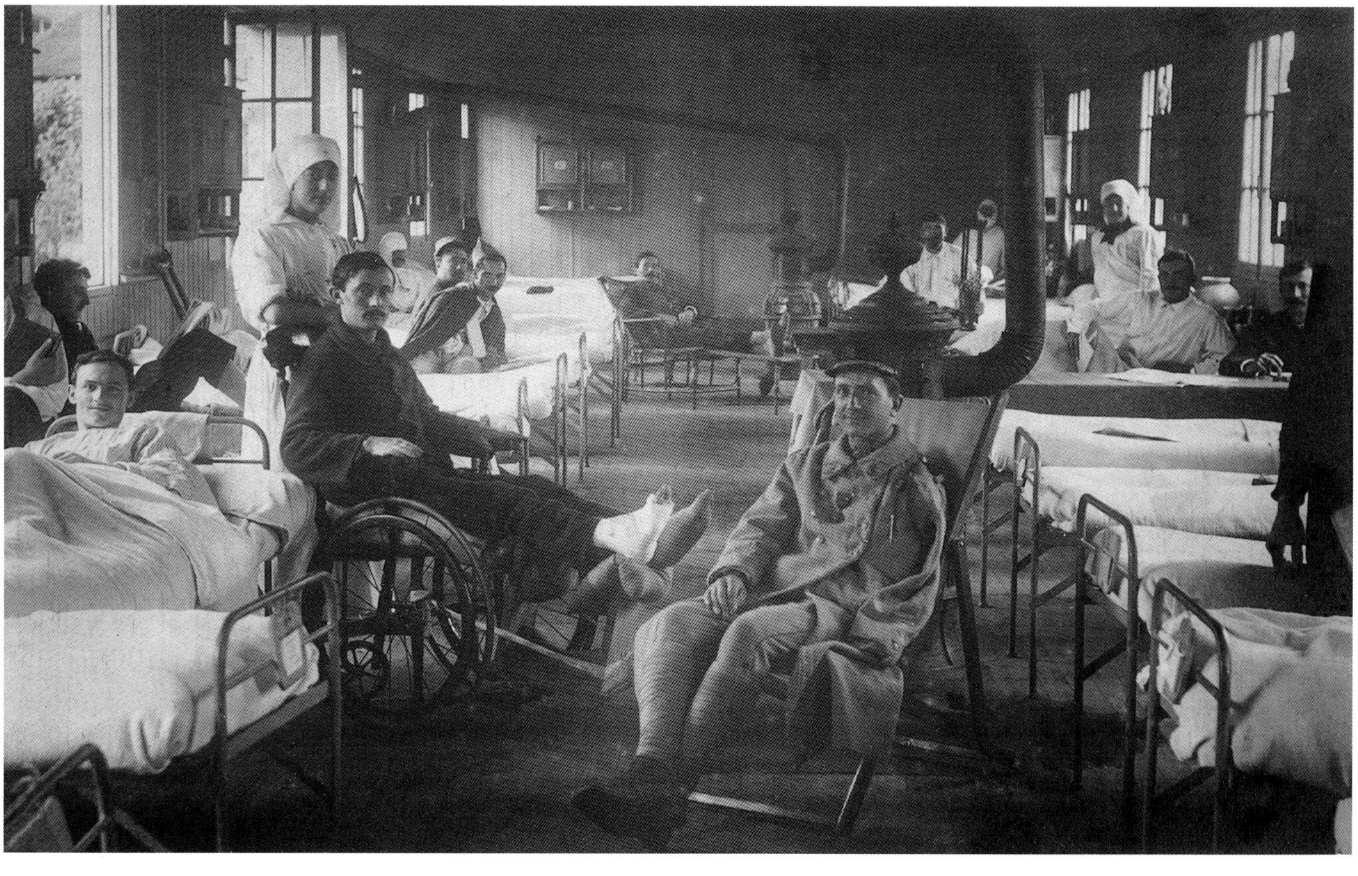

Nurses tending to the wounded in a hospital near the front. The *poilu* sitting on the chair near a heater is from *Marine d'Infanterie*, as the cloth anchors on the collar of his overcoat indicate. Also, he has been awarded the *Croix de Guerre*.

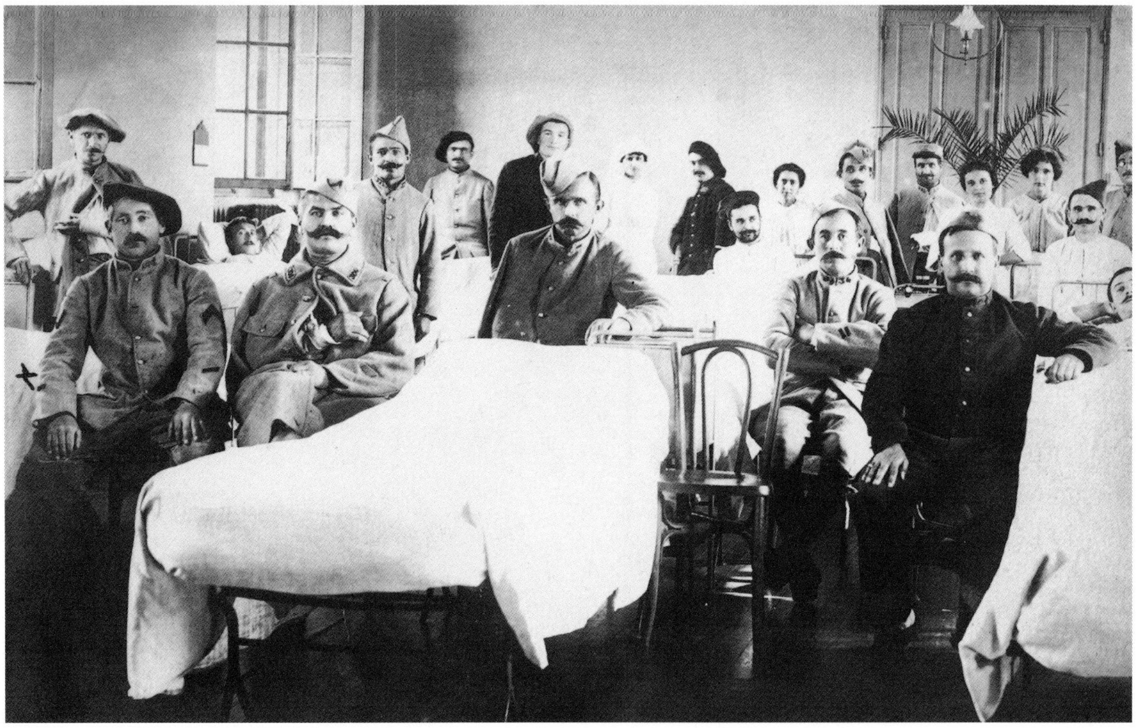

Nurses and their patients pause for a photo in a hospital near the front. The soldier in the center, wearing a dark wool beret and tunic, is a *chasseur alpin*.

Nurses pose for a group photo with *poilus* from the 146e, 74e, 31e, and other units outside a hospital.

The medics in this 1916 vintage studio wear various styles of tunics, or *vestes / tuniques/ varuese*.

Chapter Three

General Infantry

The soldier in this studio portrait wears a privately tailored double breast pocketed wool tunic and pair of trousers. The two-button wool waist belt on his tunic was a style preferred by officers and NCOs. His armlet, or *brassard*, was preferred by officers in the General Staff. The reverse side of this photo is dated August 8, 1918.

The *poilu* in this 1916 vintage studio portrait is from the 46e *Régiment*, as the cloth numbers stitched to the collar of his roughly cut wool Model 1915 horizon blue tunic and *calotte* (forage cap) indicate. In addition, he wears a cloth scarf to prevent the coarse wool from rubbing against his neck.

The mustached soldier in this studio portrait is from the 158e *Régiment*, as the metal numbers fastened to the collar of his privately tailored double breast pocketed Model 1915 horizon blue wool tunic and cloth numbers stitched to his forage cap indicate.

The mustached infantryman in this early war vintage photo wears a uniquely cut wool overcoat and single pronged waist belt. His trousers and ankle boots appear to be privately purchased.

The soldier in this studio portrait taken late in the war wears a privately tailored horizon blue wool tunic based on the Model 1915. The gold stitched numbers on his kepi and collar, as well as the bars on his sleeve, are his rank and unit distinctions. The brass buttons on his tunic bear a crossed cannon artillery motif.

The five *poilus* in this early war vintage studio photo wear a variety of cloth headdresses and unit identification numbers. The *poilu* seated in the center wears a style of beret, or *tarte*, preferred by *chasseur alpins*.

This military musician wears a dark wool uniform with cloak, or *collet*, and has gold stitched harp insignia on his collar and kepi.

The *poilu* in this 1915 vintage studio photo wears a double breast-pocketed overcoat made of coarse wool, and a cloth belt with bayonet frog for a Lebel bayonet. He is from the 125e Regiment, as the numbers on his collar indicate.

The three *poilus* in this studio photo wear issue Model 1915 horizon blue wool tunics, or *Veste Modele 1915 Bleu Horizon*, which they belted with double pronged leather belts. The cloth numbers on their collars indicate they are from the 86e Regiment.

The soldier in this studio photo holds a riding crop in his left hand, and wears a privately tailored double breast-pocketed wool tunic based on the Model 1915. The gold stitched insignia on his left sleeve was usually worn by military staff.

Underneath his Model 1915 horizon blue wool tunic, this *poilu* wears a necktie, which was a centuries old French military tradition. Owing its origin to Croatia and to the Croatian soldiers who fought in the Thirty Years War (1618-48), the necktie has been a part of the French army since the time of Louis XIV. The etymology of the French word for necktie, or *cravate*, is found in the phrase "*a la Croate*," or "*as a Croat*," thus attributing it to the style of Croatian born soldiers who served in French Hussar Regiments.

The mustached soldier in this studio photo wears a horizon blue wool tunic based on the Model 1915 with pleated breast pockets. In addition, he has two metal sixes fastened to his collar, and has been awarded the War Cross, or *Croix de Guerre*.

The mustached lieutenant in this studio portrait is from the 135e *Régiment*, and has been awarded the *Croix de Guerre*.

This soldier from the 80e *Régiment* wears a privately tailored double breast pocketed tunic that appears rather wrinkled. He has been awarded the *Croix de Guerre*, and wears an armlet (*brassard*) worn by officers in the General Staff.

The decorated *poilu* in this studio photo wears an issue Model 1915 horizon blue tunic and *calotte*, or forage cap.

This *poilu* from the 237e *Régiment* wears a privately tailored horizon blue wool tunic based on the Model 1915. On his left sleeve he has stitched service chevrons and telegraph insignia. Also, he has been decorated with the *Croix de Guerre*.

The soldier in this 1916 vintage studio photo wears a modified Model 1915 horizon blue wool tunic, which he belted with a single pronged leather belt. He has cloth numbers "155" stitched to his collar, and the same metal numbers fastened to his *calotte*.

The mustached soldier in this 1916 vintage studio portrait is in a sapper unit, as the cloth insignia on the left sleeve of his overcoat indicates. Also, he is from the 302e *Régiment*.

The *poilu* in this studio photo wears a Model 1915 horizon blue tunic, or *Veste Modele 1915 bleu horizon*, and has sapper unit insignia stitched on both his right and left sleeve.

These *poilus* are clad in pre to early war style kepis and white fatigues. Some of them are sappers, as the insignia on their left sleeve indicates.

These two soldiers are from the 158e *Régiment*, as the cloth number on their tunics, overcoats, and the soldier's kepi (right) indicates.

The three *poilus* in this studio portrait wear Model 1915 horizon blue tunics and three different styles of cloth headdress, such as a beret or *tarte* (right), kepi (center), and *calotte*, or forage cap (left). In addition, the *poilu* standing in the center is in the 69e *Régiment* and has been awarded the War Cross, or *Croix de Guerre*.

The two soldiers from the 47e *Régiment* in this 1916 vintage studio portrait wear horizon blue wool overcoats (*manteaux*) and forage caps.

These four *poilus* clad in overcoats, kepis, and early style field boots are from the 21e *Régiment*.

The *poilu* in this 1916 vintage studio photo is from the 388e *Régiment*, as the cloth numbers on his Model 1915 tunic indicate. Underneath his tunic he wears a shirt (*chemise*) and necktie, or *cravate*, a centuries old French military tradition. He wears corduroy trousers and puttees with a style of shoe normally worn around the barracks.

The *poilu* in this studio photo is from the 325e *Régiment*, as the metal numbers on his horizon bleu wool kepi, and the cloth numbers on his Model 1915 tunic indicate. He has service chevrons stitched to the upper portion of his left sleeve.

The three soldiers in this studio photo display the relaxed and civilian look that was common as the war dragged on. The soldier in the center has been awarded the *Croix de Guerre*.

This lieutenant wears a horizon blue wool Model 1915 tunic with no regimental numbers on his collar, as well as matching trousers and a forage cap.

The *poilu* in this studio photo is from the 36e *Régiment*, as the cloth numbers on his horizon blue wool Model 1915 tunic and *calot* indicate. He has two wound chevrons stitched to his right sleeve.

The decorated, white gloved officer holding a saber with sword knot in this studio photo wears a gala dress tunic and trousers.

The mustached bugler wears a tight fitting nine button dark wool waistcoat, or *ras-le-cul*, and an early style field boot. The colors of the cordage wrapped around his bugle are red, white, and blue.

This *poilu*, clutching his 8mm Lebel caliber Lebel 1886/93 bolt action rifle with bayonet, is outfitted in full gear, including an extra pair of field boots, or *brodequins*.

This lieutenant is from the 107e *Régiment*, and is armed with a 8mm Lebel caliber Lebel 1886/93 bolt action rifle and bayonet. He wears his identification bracelet on his right wrist.

This early war *poilu* from the 69e *Régiment* is armed with an 8mm Lebel caliber Lebel 1886/93 bolt action rifle and bayonet, and is clad in full battle dress. The hooks on the bayonet were later removed because of the tendency to catch on the barbed wire when bayoneting through an entanglement.

This home guardsman wears a corduroy tunic with armlet, or *brassard*. He is armed with an 8mm Lebel caliber Gras 1874/80/14 bolt action rifle.

The mustached lieutenant resting his hands on his saber is from the 402e and wears a holstered 7.65mm caliber *pistolet automatique*.

These *poilus*, clad in earlier models of kepis and overcoats, are from various units, such as the 113e and 39e. Four wear rolled wool blankets across their chests and are armed with 8mm Lebel caliber Lebel 1886/93 bolt-action rifles and bayonets.

This group of *poilus* wear various models of tunics and headdresses made from a variety of materials. Several have been awarded the War Cross, or *Croix de Guerre*.

These *poilus* are waiting to leave for the front, 1916.

This group of soldiers posing for a photo outside of a café is dressed in early war vintage uniforms. In 1915, the armed forces changed to horizon blue wool; however, many soldiers continued to wear older model uniforms.

This pre to early war vintage photo displays the size of tents, as well as the configuration of an encampment.

These *poilus* wear dark wool kepis with white fatigues/work clothes, and are holding 8mm Lebel caliber Lebel 1886/93 bolt action rifles.

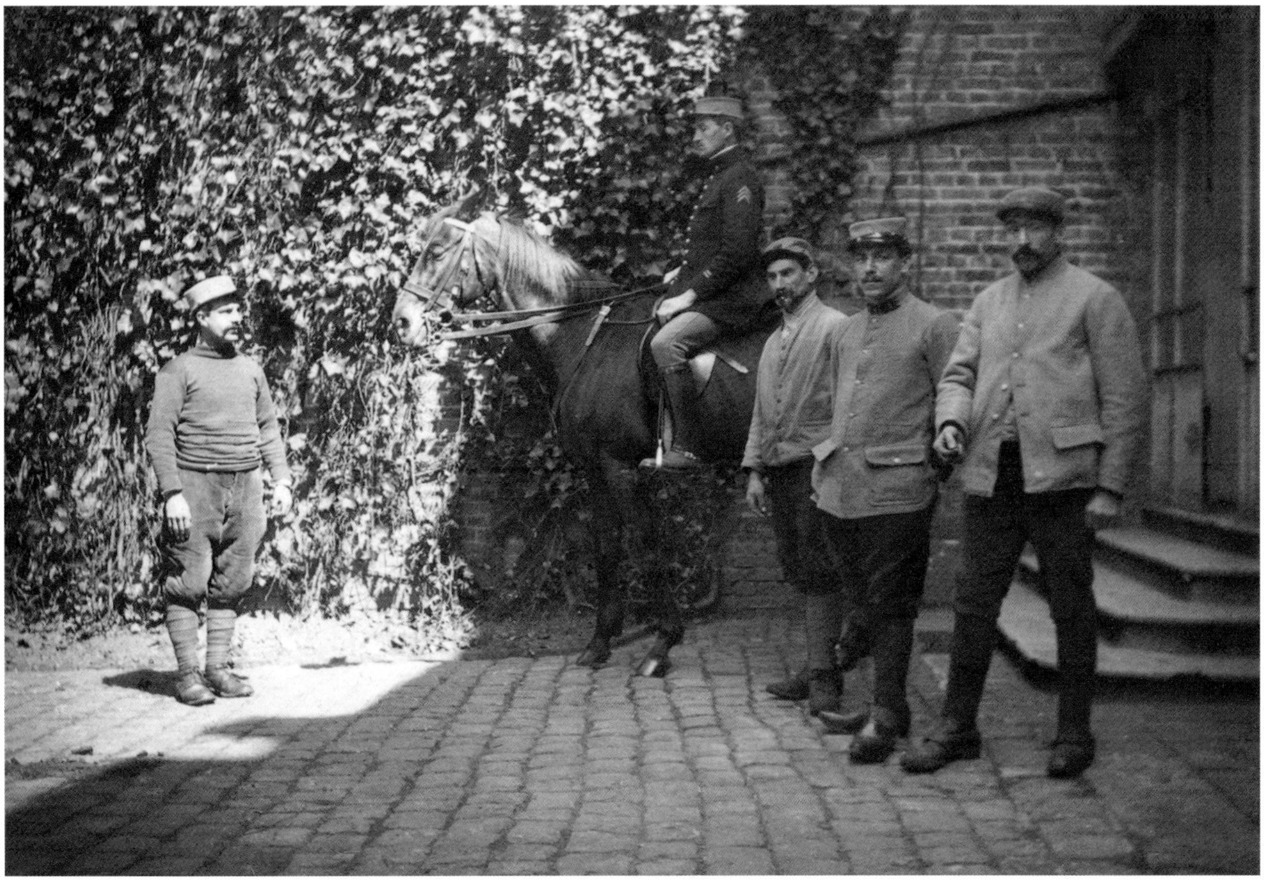

This mid to late war vintage photo taken in a French courtyard displays the various styles preferred in the armed forces. The mounted NCO in his dark wool tunic, with service chevrons on his left sleeve, the two enlisted rank soldiers in knit sweaters with corduroy trousers, and the two soldiers in Model 1915 horizon blue wool tunics were dressed in standard styles throughout the armed forces.

These *poilus*, armed with 8mm Lebel caliber Lebel 1886/93 bolt action rifles, wear white fatigues/work dress, dark wool overcoats, and kepis. Before the introduction of the M1915 Adrian helmet, soldiers wore steel skullcaps underneath their kepis.

This group of soldiers in this 1916 vintage photo are practicing for battle.

These *poilus* from the 98e *Régiment* are armed with 8mm Lebel caliber Lebel 1886/93 bolt action rifles, and are loaded with equipment, ready to move out to the front.

A group of battle weary *poilus* clad in well worn uniforms. The soldier wearing the M1915 Adrian helmet with an artillery badge has war service chevrons stitched to the left sleeve of his M1915 horizon blue wool tunic. The reverse side of this photo is dated 8/3/18.

These rugged looking soldiers are from the 122e *Régiment*, as the numbers on the collars of their battle worn M1915 horizon blue wool tunics indicate. The soldier wearing an M1915 Adrian helmet with infantry badge, seated on the right next to the lieutenant, has a wound chevron stitched to his right sleeve, and two war service chevrons stitched to his left.

These *poilus* from the 24e, as indicated by the numbers on the collars of their overcoats, are armed with 8mm Lebel caliber rifles.

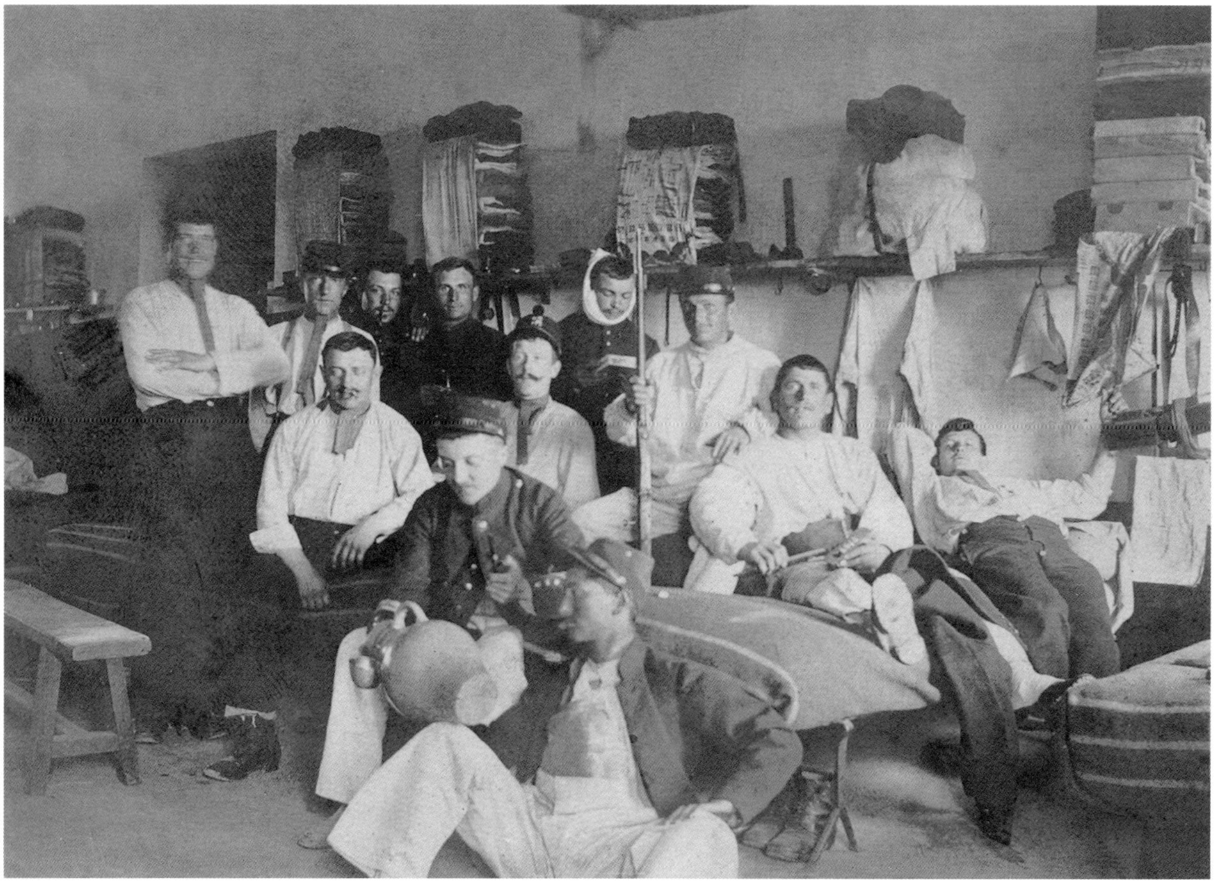

This photo offers a glimpse of early war period barracks life.

Three cigarette smoking *chasseurs* strolling on a street in Paris. Leave or furlough was very difficult to obtain for many French soldiers.

A group photo of *poilus* wearing M1915 horizon blue wool tunics pause for a photo with the bicycle and pet cat.

Three *poilus* in overcoats pause for a photo and a break, taking in the view while on leave.

An Imperial Russian officer strolling with Red Cross nurses, French officers, and other public dignitaries in Paris.

Four *poilus* from the 36e Régiment clad in corduroy tunics and field boots with leather gaiters.

These *poilus* are from the 179e *Régiment*, as the numbers on their *calottes* (forage caps) indicate. All wear white cotton drill clothing over their horizon blue wool uniforms. The rifles are 8mm Lebel caliber Model 1916 Berthier bolt-action rifles. The feed mechanism on this model was a five round clip-loaded box magazine.

These *poilus* are from the 218e *Régiment*, as the numbers stitched to the collar of their horizon blue wool overcoats indicate. This photo shows how cuts, color, and grades of material varied, even when issued to *poilus* in the same unit.

These *poilus* are from the 99e *Régiment*, as the numbers on the collars of their Model 1915 horizon blue wool tunics indicate. Their trousers vary from corduroy to horizon blue wool.

A relaxed group of *poilus* in drill clothing, lounging on and around their cots. This photo shows how chalk was used to mark and identify equipment in the barracks.

This group of *poilus* is dressed in drill clothing and wooden clogs, which were popular barracks attire. They are holding their Model 1852 tin coated metal mess kits, Model 1877 cloth covered canteens, and the regulation drinking cup.

This group of *poilus* camped near the front pauses for a photo before continuing to eat from their Model 1852 tin coated metal mess kits, or *Modele 1852 gamelles*.

These soldiers wear work fatigues and dark colored wool waist coats, or *ras le culs*, and have decided to pause from eating and drinking the contents in their various models of mess equipment to take a photo.

The *poilus* in this 1914 vintage group photo wear dark colored wool kepis and overcoats, and are armed with 8mm Lebel caliber Lebel 1886/93 bolt action rifles.

This group of *poilus*, clad in kepis and overcoats, pause for a photo before going to the front. In addition to their weapons and other equipment, each has a general-purpose cloth bag with strap flung over his right shoulder.

A mounted bugler wearing a Model 1915 horizon blue wool tunic, trousers, and kepi. This photo offers a side view of equestrian gear used during the First World War.

With 8mm Lebel caliber Lebel 1886/93 bolt action rifles and bayonets resting on their right shoulders, these *poilus* march down a dirt road behind an officer with a drawn saber.

The *poilus* in this 1914 vintage photo are clad in kepis and overcoats. Before the arrival of the Model 1915 Adrian helmet, *poilus* wore metal skullcaps underneath their kepis. They are armed with 8mm Lebel 1886/93 bolt action rifles.

This photo offers a view of camp life during the early days of the war, and some of the equipment soldiers had at their disposal, such as the collapsible waterproof canvas bucket.

In this 1914 vintage photo, this group of *poilus* stands ready for battle wearing their kepis with overcoats, and armed with 8mm Lebel 1886/93 bolt action rifles.

In addition to showing a variety of kepis and overcoats, this photo reveals how equipment was carried on a *poilu's* haversack. This photo is postmarked December 7, 1914.

These seven *poilus* clad in drill fatigues, kepis, and overcoats pose for a photo outside their tent in a camp near the front.

In a village near the front, this group of *poilus* pose for a group photo wearing horizon blue colored kepis, tent hats, and Model 1915 tunics. 1918.

This muddied and battle weary *poilu* is from the 86e *Régiment*, as the numbers on his Model 1915 horizon blue wool tunic indicate. He has two war service chevrons stitched to the left sleeve of his tunic.

This decorated NCO is from the 142e *Régiment*, as the coarse wool collar patches on his privately tailored gabardine tunic—based on the Model 1915 tunic—indicate. He wears a unique style of ankle boot that buttons on the right side of the boot.

This *poilu* is from the 272e *Régiment*, as his cloth collar patches indicate. He has been decorated with the *Croix de Guerre*.

This soldier, who is holding his regulation drinking cup, or *quart réglementaire*, is from the 134e *Régiment*, as the collar patches on his coarse wool overcoat indicate. The roll on his right shoulder kept his rifle from slipping off.

The NCO in this 1918 vintage studio photo wears a horizon blue wool tunic, and has been decorated with the War Cross, or *Croix de Guerre*.

The mustached *poilu* in this 1915 vintage studio photo taken in Paris wears a wool kepi and overcoat with his unit numbers "61" stitched to his collar. The roll on his right shoulder kept his rifle from slipping off.

This NCO is from the 119e *Régiment*, as the cloth numbers on his horizon blue wool kepi, and the metal numbers on the collar of his tunic, indicate. He has been decorated with the *Croix de Guerre*.

The mustached soldier clutching his saber in this studio photo taken in Paris wears a wool hooded cloak in addition to his wool overcoat.

This *poilu* is from the 134e *Régiment*, as the cloth numbers on the collar of his Model 1915 horizon blue wool tunic indicate. He wears a privately purchased pair of leather lace up boots, with leather flaps that buckle across the upper front half of the boot.

The *poilu* in this 1916 vintage studio photo wears a Model 1915 tunic made of coarse horizon blue wool, with his unit numbers "173" stitched to his collar. He has been decorated with the War Cross, or *Croix de Guerre*.

This soldier, resting his hands on a saber, wears a horizon blue wool kepi and a dark colored wool waist coat, or *ras le cul*, with his unit numbers "106" stitched to his collar. The reverse of this photo is dated May 1917.

The six *poilus* in this photo wear a variety of tunics and cloth headdresses. Two of the three *poilus* seated on a rock have war service chevrons stitched to the left sleeves of their Model 1915 horizon blue wool tunics. The *poilu* seated on the right has been decorated with the *Croix de Guerre*.

This is everything *le poilu* brought to and from the battle.

Chapter Four

Motor Corps

The soldier posing with his covered truck on a cobblestone road in a small village near the front is from an equipment transport team, or *Train des equipages*, which took troops and supplies to and from the front. Most trucks did not have windshields because the concussion from an explosion would shatter it. The reverse side of this photo is dated November 14, 1917.

On a muddy road en route to the front, a *poilu* wearing a Model 1915 Adrian helmet and fur collared leather jacket pauses for a photo with his spoke-wheel covered truck.

Three *poilus* pose for a photo with their spoke-wheel covered truck with removable canopy. Their transport team insignia, which depicts the silhouette of a boar standing under a tree, is painted on the tarp covering the truck. The *poilu* standing on the right is from the 131e *Régiment* and has a *Croix de Guerre* pinned to his Model 1915 horizon blue wool tunic.

On a traveled dirt road running past a woods en route to the front, drivers pause to lean against their canopied truck for a photo. The mustached driver wearing a wool beret leans against the spoke-wheel, with an electric light near his head that served as both a headlight and searchlight. The driver, wearing a *calotte* (forage cap), leans against the grill plate.

Drivers retrieving staff from their gothic quarters, 1917.

Five *poilus* from the 102e and 131e regiments pose for a photo with their staff car in their *calottes* and Model 1915 tunics on their way to the front.

Left: This mustached ambulance driver, as indicated by the "A" on his cloth armlet, or brassard, leans proudly against his vehicle for a photo wearing his horizon blue wool overcoat and kepi. 1918.

Below: Four *poilus* clad in early war garments pause for a photo with their battle-worn supply truck on a heavily traveled road en route to the front. Such trucks were used in great numbers on the road from Bar le Duc to Verdun, which came to be known as "*La Voie Sacree*," or "The Sacred Road." "*La Voie Sacree*," or "*La Route*," as it was referred to by most *poilus*, was a vital military route for the French Army, because it was the only means of supply after the railway lines were destroyed by German artillery.

Mechanics in cotton fatigues and drivers in horizon blue wool pose for a photo in front of their covered trucks in Marseille. The reverse of this photo is dated 1915.

These seven *poilus* clad in dark wool waist coats (*ras le culs*) and Model 1915 tunics pose for a photo in front of a row of covered trucks preparing to tow 155mm caliber Bange heavy artillery pieces to the front.

This group of *poilus* in this 1917 vintage photo pose for a photo with a spoke-wheel open bed truck. The canvas roof covering the driver's compartment was stretched over a metal frame and could be folded back.

On a road near a cottage in the French countryside, a group of *poilus* pause for a photo with their spoke-wheel truck. The engine hood has been removed, as well as the canopy for the driver's compartment.

This group is from the *Train Matériel* 214, as indicated by the painted "TM 214" on the round sign and the stenciling on the side of the truck on the far right. July 14, 1917.

Mechanics and drivers pose for a photo with their spoke-wheel covered trucks on a dirt road heading to the front, 1917.

Medical staff and ambulance drivers pose for a group photo in front of their covered ambulance truck. Several of the drivers wear an armband (*brassard*) on their right sleeve with the letter "A" for ambulance.

This *poilu*, wearing a kepi and horizon blue wool uniform, stands alongside a camouflaged Model 1913 De Dion Bouton automobile with 75mm cannon, or *l' auto canon de 75 De Dion Bouton modéle 1913*. This Model 1913 De Dion Bouton was used as an anti-aircraft weapon, or as an infantry support vehicle.

Two drivers in a row of equipment transport team (*Train des equipages*) trucks headed to the front.

Allied medical transport unit, 1917.

This group of *poilus*, clad in various models of kepis, overcoats, and tunics, display a truck wheel.

On a traveled dirt road lined with trees, *poilus* clad in various headdresses, tunics, and overcoats line up with their spoke-wheel covered trucks for a photo. The unit insignia depicts a butterfly, and is painted on the front of each truck above the driver's compartment.

This mechanic, wearing work fatigues, shows how to fill a tire, 1916.

Chapter Five

Artillery

These four artillerists are from the 13e *Régiment*, as the numbers stitched to the collars of their nine button dark wool waistcoats, or *ras le cul*, indicate. The spurs on the heels of their boots indicate they are mounted artillery. They pose proudly for a photo with a Model 1878 155mm caliber De Bange heavy artillery piece with ramps behind its wheels, which helped absorb the impact of the recoil when fired. The equally spaced apart flat wood blocks that are fastened to the wheels are known as "*ceinture de roués*."

These artillerists pose for a photo with their Model 1877 155mm caliber De Bange heavy artillery piece near a wood. They are clad in dark wool kepis and nine button waistcoats (*ras le cul*), and have their unit number "43" stitched on both.

These artillerists clad in dark wool nine button waistcoats pose for a photo in the field with their caisson and 75mm field cannon, or *le canon de 75*.

These five artillerists, posed with their 75mm field cannon (*le canon de 75*) wear dark wool kepis and waistcoats (*ras le cul*) bearing their unit numbers.

Eleven artillerists clad in dark wool kepis and nine button waistcoats (*ras le cul*) pose proudly with their armor shielded 75mm field cannon, or *le canon de 75*. Some of these artillerists have spurs on their boots, indicating they are from a mounted or horse artillery unit.

These *poilus* are from *105e Artillerie* and have wheeled their cannon from its firing position, opened its breech, and placed seven artillery rounds by it for this group photo.

These artillerists are from the *37e Régiment Artillerie, 68e Batterie*, and have decided to pose for a group photo with their 75mm field cannon, or *le canon de 75*. The lieutenant standing on the far left holding a pipe has two war service chevrons stitched to the left sleeve of his Model 1915 horizon blue wool tunic. The seated lieutenant with his kepi resting on an artillery round, has a wound chevron stitched to the right sleeve of his dark wool tunic, and has been awarded the War Cross, or *Croix de Guerre*.

This group of artillerists poses with their Model 1877 90mm De Bange field cannon while on maneuvers.

Sixteen artillerists wearing dark wool kepis and nine button *ras le cul* pose for a photo with their *le canon de 75*.

Artillerists clad in dark wool *ras le cul* and cotton fatigues cluster around their field cannon for a photo.

Five of the six artillerists wear various interpretations of Model 1915 horizon blue wool tunics, while the sixth wears a knit turtleneck sweater. This 1917 vintage photo offers a breech view of a firing position on the frontlines.

Seven artillerists wearing dark blue wool kepis and cotton fatigues pose with their 75mm field cannon, or *le canon de 75*.

Six artillerists wearing Adrian helmets (Casques Adrian) with artillery badges pose for a photo in the field with their caisson and cannon.

These *poilus* are from the 82e *Régiment*, as the numbers on their collars indicate. They pose for this group photo in front of a Model 1877 155mm caliber De Bange heavy artillery piece.

Twelve artillerists clad in various models of tunics pose by their Model 1877 155mm caliber De Bange heavy artillery piece. Cannons with older, or Napoleonic style carriages were often re-laid after firing.

A group of artillerists wearing Model 1915 horizon blue wool tunics pose for a photo with their 75mm field canon, or *le canon de 75*.

Fifteen artillerists wearing cotton fatigues pose for a photo with four Model 1877 80mm caliber artillery pieces.

Above: This is a commercially reproduced period photo from a series documenting the Great War.

Right: This mustached artillerist poses for a photo next to a Model 1877 155mm caliber De Bange heavy artillery piece wearing a horizon blue wool kepi and tunic.

This photo offers a breech view of a firing position covered with an arched piece of corrugated metal. The artillerist stands near an opening in the wood plank floor for shell casings. Winter 1917.

This decorated artillerist places his hat atop a shell for heavy caliber railway or naval artillery pieces.

A *poilu* wearing a horizon blue wool uniform rests his hand on a heavy caliber artillery round. He has service chevrons stitched to the left sleeve of his tunic based on the Model 1915.

The mounted artillerist in this pre to early war studio photo is from the 25e *Régiment*, as the numbers on his dark wool tunic with seven braids and kepi indicate.

The artillerist clutching his saber in this pre to early war studio photo is from the 51e *Régiment*, as the numbers on the collar of his dark wool tunic indicate.

A breech view of a 240mm trench mortar, 1916.

Two *poilus* clad in horizon blue wool uniforms observing a 240mm trench mortar, 1917.

This Field cannon has been set upon a rotating mount, enabling it to be fired from various positions.

A 58mm trench mortar, 1917.

Transporting heavy artillery through a wooded area, 1917.

Artillerists transport heavy artillery through a muddy wooded area, 1917.

Entrenching heavy artillery, 1917.

This photo was taken by an American soldier (Doughboy), and displays a *poilu* standing next to a destroyed battery.

Captured battery, 1918

Destroyed battery, 1918

Camouflaged railway cannon, 1917.

Firing a railway gun, 1917.

Camouflaged railway cannon, 1917.

War trophies on display in Paris, 1918-19.

Chapter Six

Model 1915 Adrian Helmets

These three *poilus* from the 71e *Régiment* wear Model 1915 Adrian helmets painted with a matt finish. The second lieutenant is armed with an 8mm caliber Lebel rifle and is outfitted in full battle dress.

This mustached soldier is from the 6e *Régiment*, as the cloth numbers on his double breast pocketed horizon blue wool overcoat indicate. Fastened to his matt finish horizon blue Model 1915 Adrian helmet is an infantry badge.

The stitched bars near the right cuff on this soldier's horizon blue wool tunic indicate his rank is colonel. He is from the 37e *Régiment*, as the numbers on his collar indicate, and he is in the infantry, as revealed by the badge on his Model 1915 Adrian helmet. This photo is dated 1917.

The mounted *poilu* is from the 12e *Régiment*, as the cloth numbers on the collar of his Model 1915 horizon blue wool tunic indicate. He has a matt finish on his Model 1915 Adrian helmet, and is armed with a saber and an 8mm Lebel caliber Model 1892 Berthier artillery carbine, the bayonet for which he has in its scabbard, hanging from his leather waist belt.

The second lieutenant, resting his hands on the muzzle of his 8mm Lebel rifle, has belted his horizon blue wool overcoat with an early model waist belt. The leather ammo pouches on his waist belt appear to be an earlier model, or of foreign manufacture. His gloss finish Model 1915 Adrian helmet bears either an administration or a medical badge.

This mustached soldier is from the 86e *Régiment*, as the cloth numbers stitched to the collars of his horizon blue wool overcoat and Model 1915 tunic indicate. In addition, he has an artillery badge fastened to his Model 1915 Adrian helmet.

These two *poilus* wear Model 1915 Adrian helmets painted horizon blue with a matt finish. Instead of a tunic, they have chosen to wear an issue style *chemise*, or shirt. Each has a *musette* (bread bag) flung over his shoulder.

The *poilu* in this 1916 vintage studio photo is from the 147e *Régiment*, as cloth numbers stitched to the collar of his overcoat indicate. His Model 1915 Adrian helmet has a very rough finish, usually caused by exposure to the conditions in the trenches and on the battlefield.

The *poilu* in this studio photo wears a Model 1915 Adrian helmet with an infantry badge. He has the numbers "404" stitched to his collar, and an artillery distinction stitched to the left arm of his overcoat below his armlet, or *brassard*. The lower pockets on his overcoat are a different color and grade of wool, indicating they were added later.

The soldier posing with his family in this 1917 vintage studio photo wears a Model 1915 Adrian helmet with an infantry badge and leather chinstrap, or *jugulaire*. He has his unit numbers "22" stitched to the collar, and a service chevron stitched to the left sleeve of his overcoat. Below his service chevron he wears an issue stamped medic's armband.

The *poilu* from the 22e *Régiment* in this studio photo wears a Model 1915 horizon blue wool tunic that he has belted with a two pronged buckle leather belt. His Model 1915 Adrian helmet, with an infantry badge and leather chinstrap, or *jugulaire*, rests on a leather covered photo album on a pedestal.

The lieutenant holding his Model 1915 Adrian helmet with an infantry badge and leather chinstrap (*jugulaire*) wears a coarse wool tunic based on the Model 1915. He has the number four stitched to his collar, and he wears a starched cotton collar guard to keep the wool from rubbing his neck.

This *poilu*, holding his Model 1915 Adrian helmet, or *Casque Adrian*, under his right arm, wears an issue Model 1915 horizon blue wool tunic with the cloth numbers "33" stitched to his collar.

The mustached lieutenant from the 369e *Régiment* in this 1917 vintage studio photo wears an overcoat made of coarse wool with two breast pockets. His Model 1915 Adrian helmet, with an infantry badge and *jugulaire*, rests on a wood chair.

Clad in their Model 1915 Adrian helmets and armed with 8mm Lebel rifles, the soldiers of the 44e *Régiment* smile for the camera as they march down a dirt road en route to the frontlines. Three of the smiling soldiers have wound chevrons stitched to their right sleeves.

With their rolled wool blankets across their chests and the leather straps of their rifles and wool covered canteens flung over their shoulders, these *poilus* wearing Model 1915 Adrian helmets cast a glance at the camera as they march down a narrow dirt path.

Wearing kepis, overcoats, tunics, and Model 1915 Adrian helmets, soldiers from the 83e *Régiment* pose for a group photo. Three of these soldiers do not have any badges on their Model 1915 Adrian helmets, while others have artillery badges fastened to the front above the visor.

Poilus from the 150e *Régiment* pose for a group photo in a field near the front. With the exception of the officer wearing a dark wool kepi, the others wear Model 1915 Adrian helmets with infantry badges and leather chinstraps.

Clad in Model 1915 Adrian helmets and horizon blue wool tunics, this group of *poilus* poses for a group photo outside their barracks, 1917.

Standing near a guard house painted in the French national colors, this group of *poilus* poses for a photo wearing dark wool kepis and Model 1915 Adrian helmets with gloss finish.

Near a wood dwelling surrounded by undergrowth, six *poilus* wearing Model 1915 Adrian helmets and horizon blue wool uniforms pose proudly for a photo with their 8mm Lebel rifles across their backs. The rectangular painted metal canisters they carry contain their gasmasks.

A group of *poilus* wearing Model 1915 Adrian helmets and work fatigues pause for a photo while on maneuvers.

A group of *poilus* from the 21e *Régiment* pose for a photo clad in Model 1915 horizon blue wool tunics and Adrian helmets with artillery badges. The mustached NCO wearing a Model 1915 horizon blue wool tunic and kepi is from the 20e *Régiment*, and has been awarded the War Cross, or *Croix de Guerre*.

The group of *poilus* in this 1917 vintage photo wear Model 1915 Adrian helmets and horizon blue wool tunics. The soldier seated in the first row, next to the one holding a dog, is wearing a Red Cross armband on the left sleeve of his tunic. Walking sticks or canes, such as those seen here, were popular among *poilus*.

This group of *poilus* wearing overcoats and Model 1915 Adrian helmets display a bit of humor in this 1917 vintage photo.

Poilus from the 171e *Régiment* pose for a humorous photo outside of their barracks. The manner in which the *poilu* on the right wears his Model 1915 Adrian helmet offers a side view of the helmet.

These *poilus*, wearing Model 1915 Adrian helmets and work fatigues, rest their hands atop their sabers before receiving a blessing.

This group of *poilus* clad in Model 1915 Adrian helmets, horizon blue wool tunics, overcoats, and work fatigues pose for a photo with their musical instruments and entrenching tools.

In a sandbag reinforced dugout near the front lines, a group of *poilus* from the 121e *Régiment* pose for a photo wearing Model 1915 Adrian helmets and horizon blue wool tunics.

A group of poilus wearing Model 1915 Adrian helmets and kepis pose for a photo on an ivy covered stair of a chateau.

Five battle weary *poilus* armed with 8mm Lebel rifles pose for a photo before returning to the front.

Poilus from the 51e *Régiment* wearing Model 1915 Adrian helmets, forage caps, and/or kepis pose for a photo outside their barracks.

These nine *poilus*, wearing Model 1915 Adrian helmets with a gloss finish, are from the 152e *Régiment*, as the cloth numbers on their overcoats indicate. All nine are armed with an 8mm Lebel caliber bolt-action Berthier Model 1916 Infantry Rifle.

These *poilus* wearing Model 1915 Adrian helmets, as well as the one wearing a *calotte*, or forage cap, are from 151éme *Régiment d'Infanterie de Ligne*, as the cloth insignia on the collar of their overcoats indicate. Two of the *poilus* have bicyclist insignia stitched to the left sleeve of their Model 1915 horizon blue wool tunics.

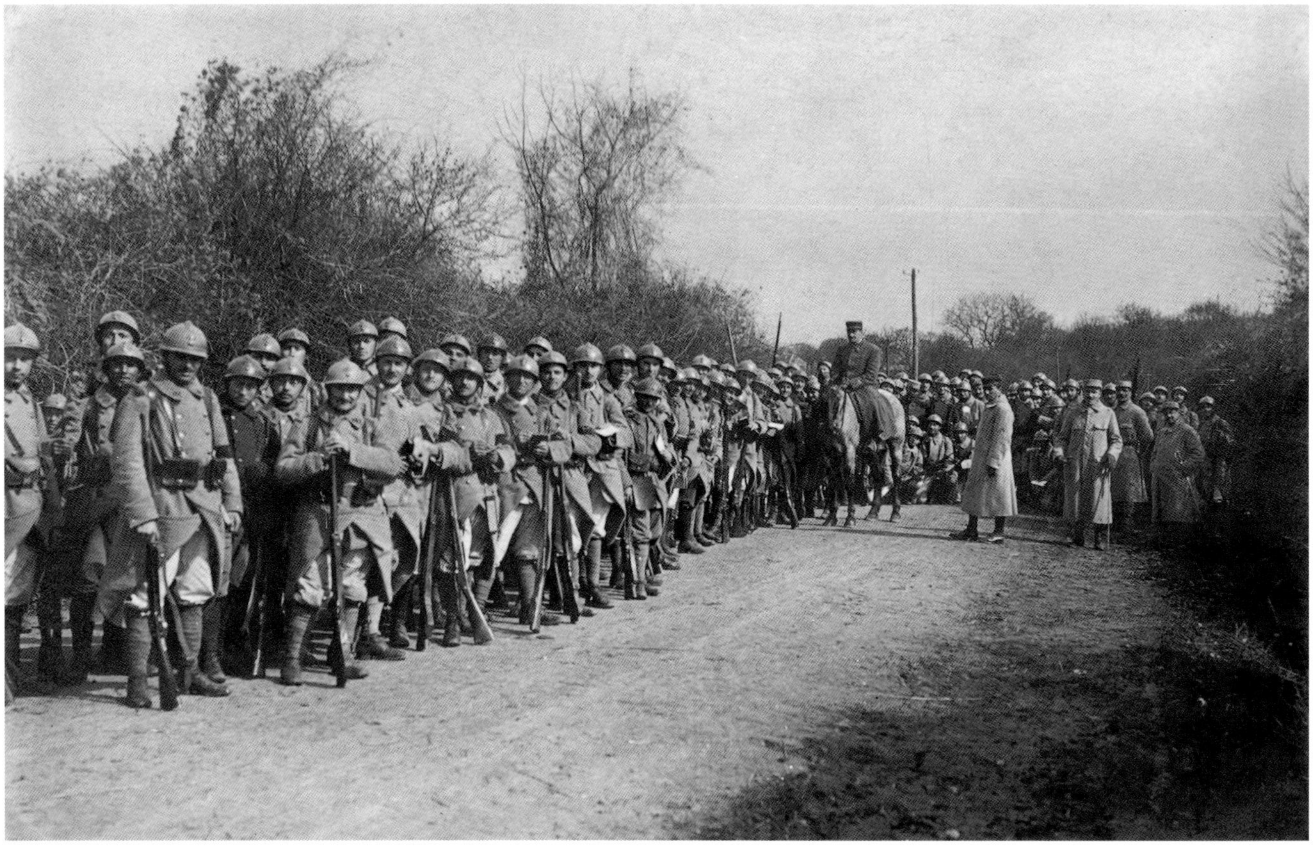

On a dirt road en route to the front, a company of *poilus* clad in Model 1915 Adrian helmets and kepis pause for a photo.

A group of *poilus* wearing Model 1915 Adrian helmets with engineer insignia pose for a photo with their commanding officers, who are wearing dark wool kepis. They are armed with 8mm Lebel caliber Model 1892 Berthier artillery carbines, or *mousqueton d'artillerie*.

Two mustached officers in Model 1915 Adrian helmets walking down a well-traveled road to the frontlines.

Five *poilus* in Model 1915 Adrian helmets and horizon blue wool tunics and overcoats pose for a photo by a stone wall.

Near a battle-damaged dwelling, five *poilus* clad in Model 1915 Adrian helmets and various models of tunics and footwear pose for a photo.

In this 1918 vintage photo, eight *poilus* wearing Model 1915 Adrian helmets and horizon blue wool tunics and overcoats pose for a photo outside of a dwelling in a forest.

A group of poilus from the 105e *Régiment*, as the cloth numbers on their overcoats indicate, pose for a photo wearing Model 1915 Adrian helmets with infantry insignia. The commanding officer in the center wears a dark wool kepi bearing the regiment numbers.

This group of *poilus* ready for battle poses for a photo wearing Model 1915 Adrian helmets and horizon blue wool tunics. The cloth numbers "35" stitched to their collars indicate their unit.

Eighteen *poilus* from the 224e *Régiment* pose for a group photo wearing Model 1915 Adrian helmets and kepis.

This group of *poilus* clad in Model 1915 Adrian helmets pose for a group photo armed with 8mm Lebel caliber Model 1916 Berthier and Model 1886/93 Lebel bolt action rifles.

Theses *poilus* wearing Model 1915 Adrian helmets are from the 39e *Régiment*, as the numbers on the collars of the horizon blue wool overcoats indicate. They are armed with 8mm Lebel caliber Berthier rifles and carbines.

Military bandsmen, along with soldiers from other branches of service, pose for a group photo wearing Model 1915 Adrian helmets and various styles of headdress.

A group of *poilus* in glossy Model 1915 Adrian helmets from the 105e *Régiment* pose for a photo in a field with their 8mm Hotchkiss machine guns.

A group of *poilus* wearing Model 1915 Adrian helmets and overcoats pose for a photo armed with 8mm Lebel caliber Model 1916 Berthier rifles. The numbers "46" on their collars indicate their unit.

This group of *poilus* clad in Model 1915 Adrian helmets and horizon blue wool tunics pose for a photo armed with 8mm Lebel caliber Model 1916 Berthier rifles.

The *poilus* in this 1917 vintage group photo wear Model 1915 Adrian helmets and dark wool kepis. The numbers "35" stitched to the collar of the horizon blue wool overcoats indicate their unit.

A group of *poilus* wearing Model 1915 Adrian helmets and horizon blue wool overcoats pose for a group photo in a railroad yard.

Twelve *poilus* pose for a photo outside of their barracks wearing Model 1915 Adrian helmets with infantry badges and nightshirts.

Chapter Seven

Air Service

A fabulous photo of four Breguet 14s flying over the front.

This photo is titled "Captain Guynemer in Full Flight."

Inspecting a Breguet 16 before a flight.

This group of *poilus* is inspecting a plane after a crash landing.

This photo of the battlefields in France was taken from a Farman pusher biplane.

An aerial view of the battlefield taken by a photographer in a Farman pusher biplane.

Two aviators pose for a photo on a snow-covered runway with their Farman pusher biplane, 1917

On a snowy runway, two aviators wearing kepis pose for a photo with their Farman pusher biplane, 1917.

Two aviators pose for a photo manning their machineguns in their Caproni C.E.P.2. The Caproni C.E.P.2 was a heavy bomber powered by 150 Hp engines.

Ground crew and pilots pushing a Farman pusher biplane across a snow-covered field, 1917.

Farman pusher biplanes parked on a snow-covered field outside of a hangar, 1917

Farman pusher biplanes parked on a snow-covered field, 1917.

A Farman pusher biplane and crewmen on a snow-covered field in 1917.

Farman pusher biplanes underneath the metal framework of a hangar, 1917.

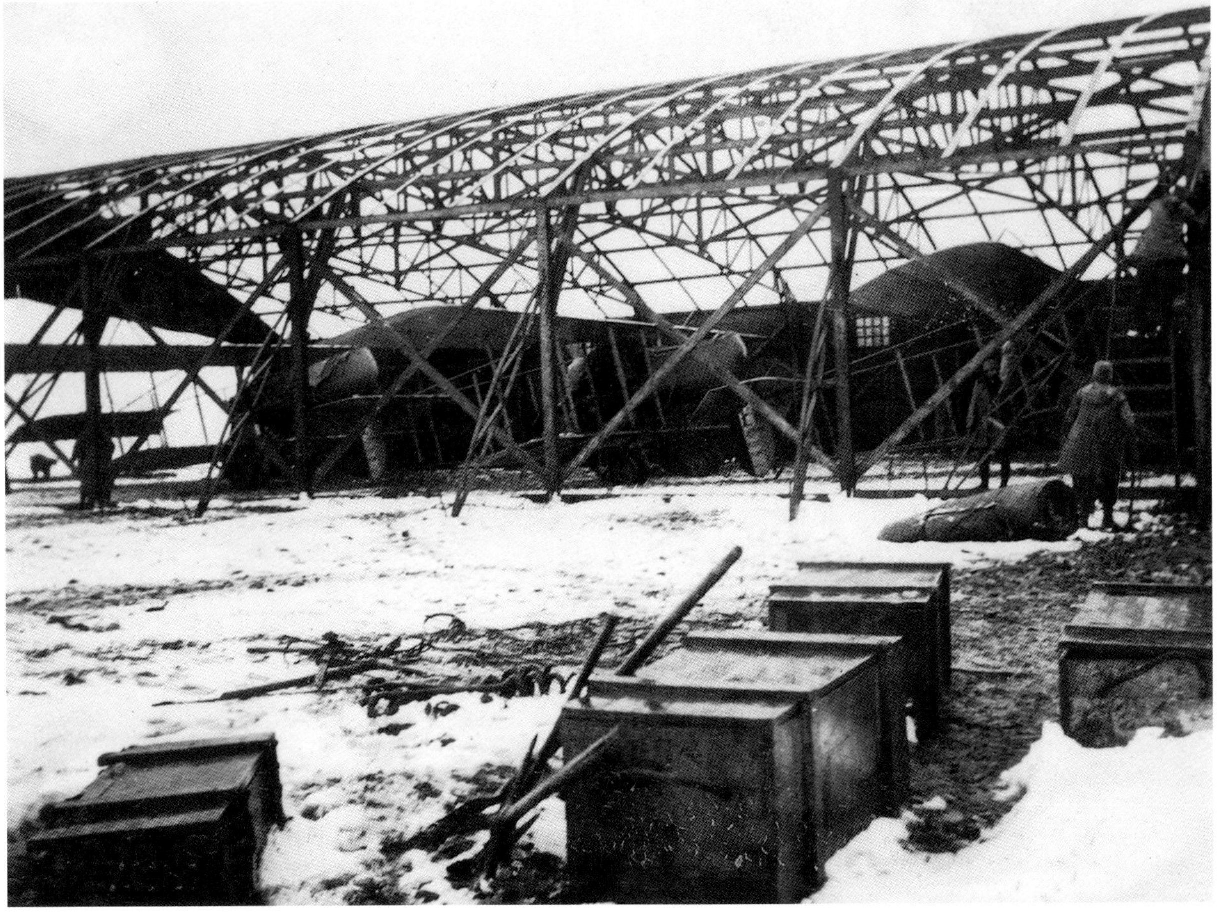

Farman pusher biplanes underneath the metal framework of a hangar, 1917.

Guiding a Farman pusher biplane into a hangar, 1917.

Guiding a Farman pusher biplane into a hangar, 1917.

A rear view of a SPAD S-7 parked on a field. The SPAD S-7 could reach a maximum speed of 120mph /192kmh.

A Caudron G.3 in flight.

Four *poilus* pose proudly for a photo with their Blériot 11 reconnaissance plane.

A group of *poilus* and civilians pose for a photo with a Blériot 11 reconnaissance plane.

This pilot, clad in his leather flight cap and jacket with fur collar, poses for a late war vintage photo holding the propeller of his Breguet 14 B2.

A Gourdou-Lesseurre C1 parked on a dirt runway, 1917.

A Farman pusher biplane on display in the War Museum in Paris, France, 1914-15.

A captured German Taube on display in the War Museum in Paris, France, 1914-15.

Three crewmen clad in kepis and work fatigues pose for a photo with their Farman F.40.

Crewmen inspecting a Nieuport biplane parked in a field.

A pilot and crewmen pause for a photo with their Nieuport biplanes parked inside a hangar. Note the roundels on the propeller.

Nieuport biplanes parked inside a hangar.

A group of *poilus* gathering around a captured Albatross D3. Fur coats were popular with aviators.

A group of *poilus* gathering around a captured Albatross D3.

Pilots, crewmen, and their planes at an aerodrome near the front.

Two *poilus* pose for a photo in the wreckage of an aircraft hangar after a bombing.

This pilot was forced to land his Breguet 14 A2 in a grassy field upside down, 1918.

Pilots and ground crew pose for a photo with their biplane, which overturned while attempting to land. 1918.

An overturned Breguet 14 biplane.

This aviator, clad in a fur-lined flight suit, poses proudly for a photo with his Farman pusher biplane before take off, 1916.

The aviator on the left, with his faithful spotted canine companion standing between his legs, wears an early model Roold flight helmet. The *poilu* on the right, with his sweetheart holding his arm, wears a Model 1915 Adrian helmet.

A group of *poilus* clad in wool kepis and tunics pose for a photo with an observation balloon in the background.

Examining the tailpiece from a demolished biplane.

The mangled remains of a biplane after a crash.

This pilot landed the nose of his Breguet 14 biplane in a grassy field.

The tailpiece of a Breguet 14.

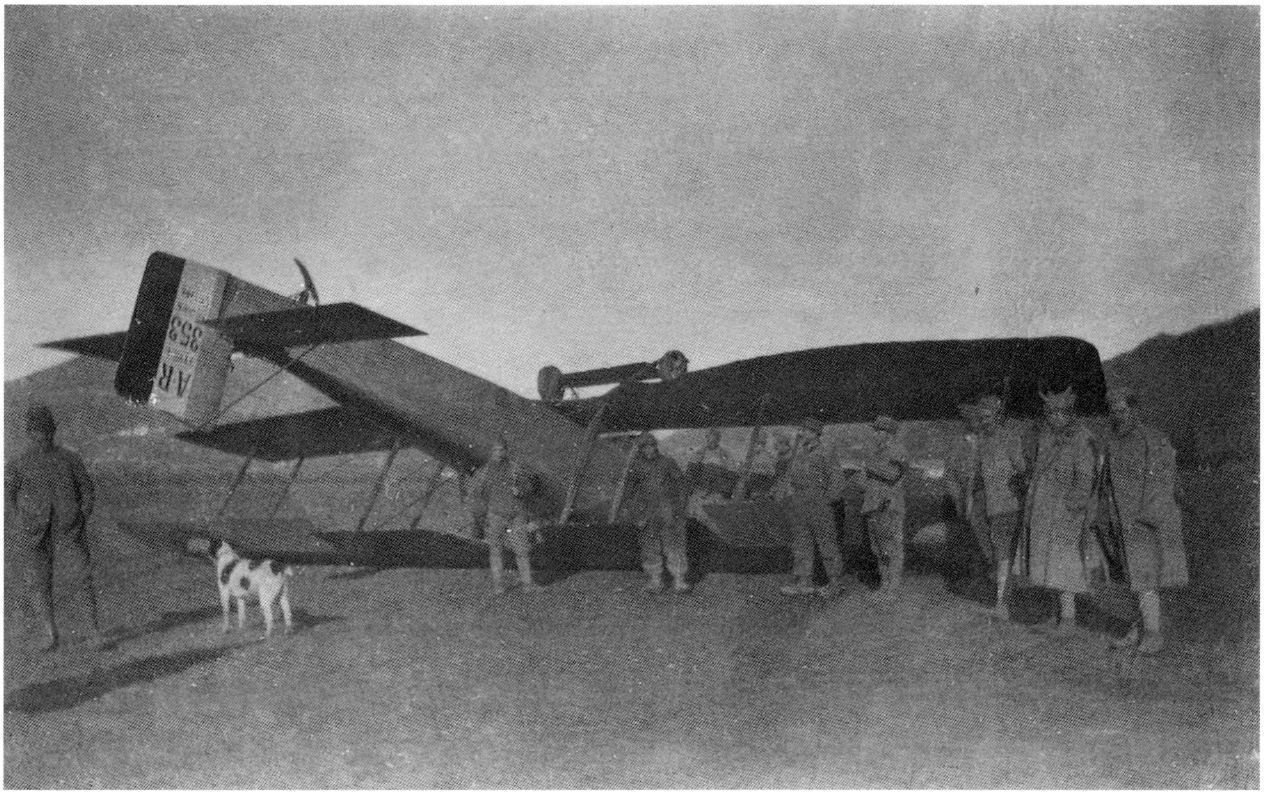

A pilot and ground crew pose for a photo with their A.R. 1 after a crash landing, 1917.

A pilot poses for a photo with his A.R. 1 after a crash landing, 1917.

This pilot landed his Salmson 2 upside down.

A pilot and ground crew pose for a photo with their Breguet 14 B2 after a crash landing, 1917.

Pilots and ground crew pose for a photo with their biplane after a crash landing, 1917.

Pilots and crew examine twin-engine biplane that crash landed in a field.

The wreckage of a Nieuport 82 after a crash landing.

Examining the wreckage of a Nieuport 82 after a crash landing.

Examining the wreckage after a crash landing.

Examining the wreckage after a crash landing.

Examining the wreckage after a crash landing.

Examining the wreckage after a crash landing.

Five *poilus* wearing horizon blue wool kepis and tunics pose for a photo with a wingless canvas fuselage.

Aviators in parade gala preparing to be decorated.

This *poilu*, who has been decorated with the *Croix de Guerre*, poses proudly with three aerial torpedoes weighing 100, 50, and 12 kilograms.

This mustached pilot wearing a kepi poses proudly for a photo in his open-air cockpit before take off.

These two soldiers wear privately tailored double breast-pocketed wool tunics with air service insignia stitched to their collars. The soldier on the left has an observer badge fastened to the flap of his left breast pocket.

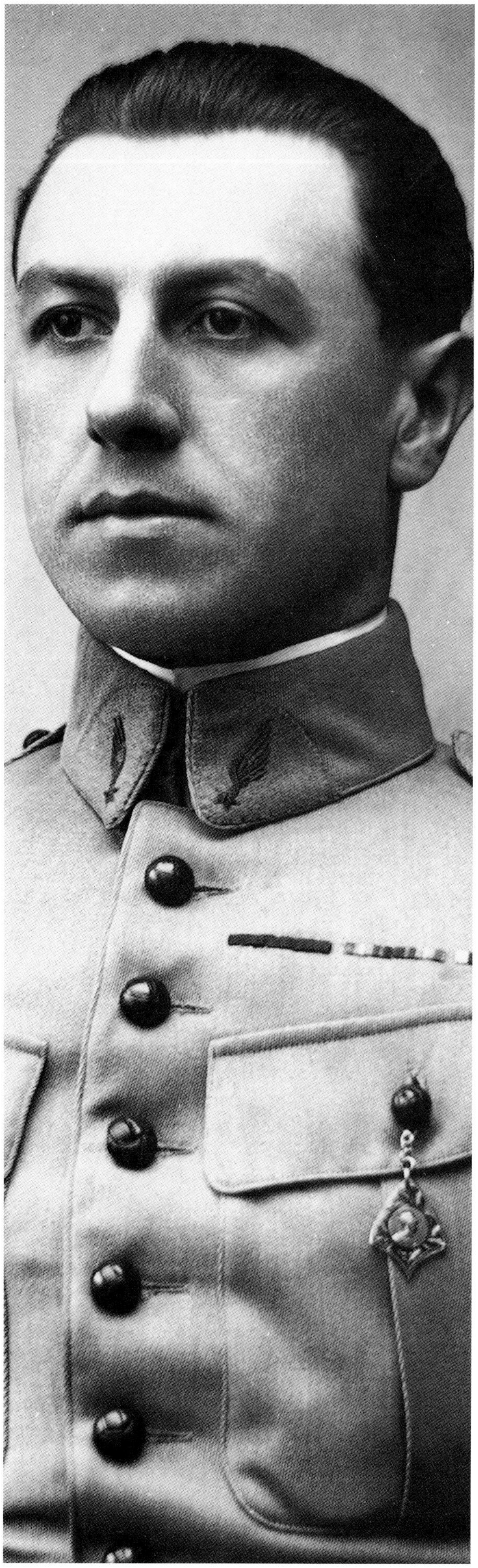

The aviator in this late war vintage studio photo wears a privately tailored horizon blue wool tunic, and has a flight badge fastened above his left breast pocket.

An aviator in a privately tailored horizon blue tunic.

Ten *poilus* pause from their work for a photo with their plane.

The *poilu* in this studio photo wears a privately tailored horizon blue wool tunic with air service insignia on his collar and a mechanic's patch on his left sleeve.

Farman pusher biplane after a crash landing on a snow covered field, January 18, 1917.

The mangled remains of a Farman pusher biplane after a crash landing on a snowy field, January 18, 1917.

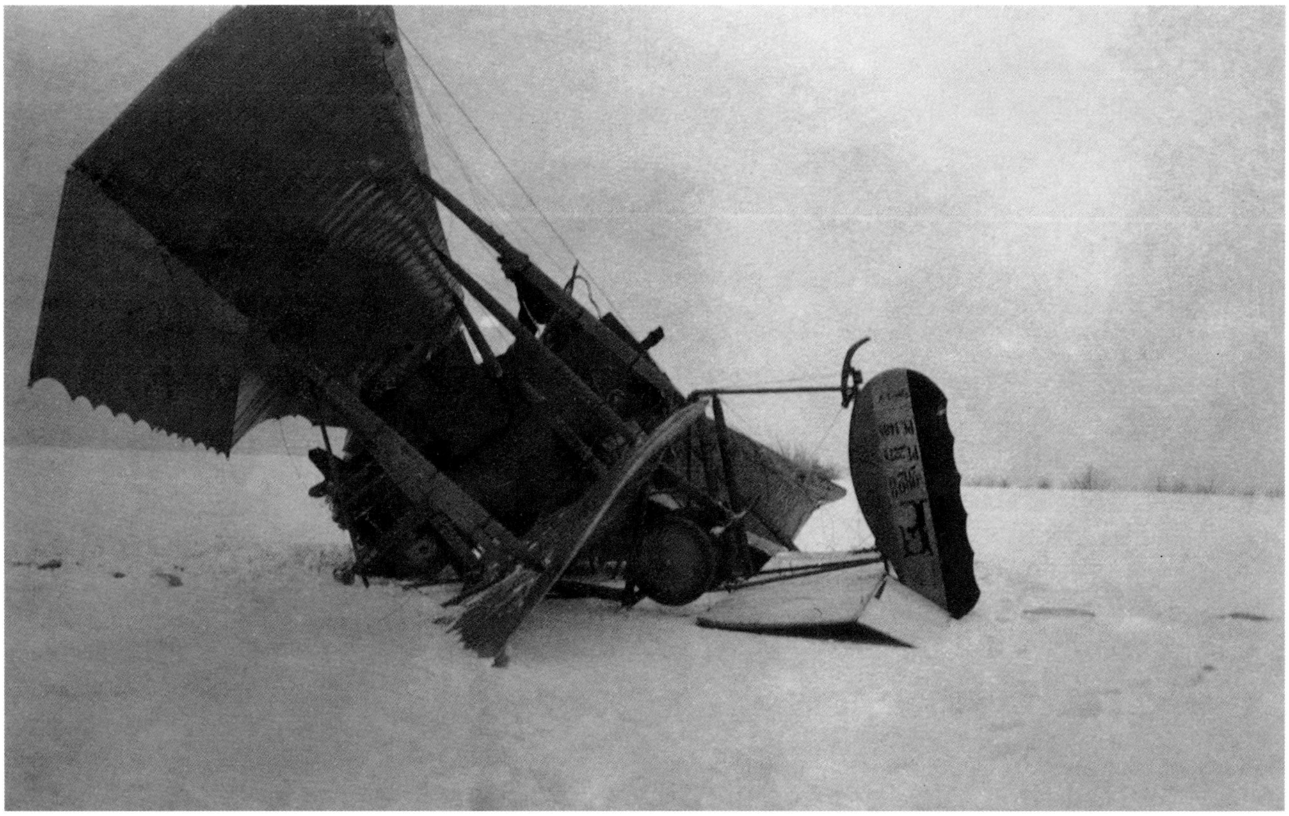

A Farman pusher biplane after a crash landing on a snowy field, January 18, 1917.

The wreckage of a Farman pusher biplane after a crash landing on a snow covered field, January 18, 1917.

The twisted wreckage of a Farman pusher biplane after a crash landing on a snowy field, January 18, 1917.

A Farman pusher biplane after a crash landing on a snow covered field, January 18, 1917.

Pilot and crew preparing their Farman pusher biplane on a snow-dusted field, January 25, 1917.

Five Imperial Germans clad in *Feldgrau* (Field Gray) pose for a photo after examining the wreckage of a downed French pilot, as the caption indicates.

Chapter Eight

Infanterie Coloniale / Infanterie Marine

Two marine infantry troopers, or *infanterie de marine*. The one on the left is dressed in a horizon blue wool tunic, with a service chevron and mechanic insignia stitched to his left sleeve. The other wears a white cotton cap with red pompom.

The marine infantryman in this 1917 vintage studio portrait wears a double-breasted coarse wool tunic with two anchors and two sixes stitched to his collar. He has an anchor stitched to his *calotte* (tent hat), which is made of the same grade of wool as his tunic.

These men are from the armored cruiser *Léon Gambetta*, as the bands on their caps with pompoms indicate. After a chase, the royal and imperial Austro-Hungarian submarine U5, or *k.u.k. Kriegsmarine U-boot U5*, torpedoed *Léon Gambetta* near Santa Maria di Luca. *Léon Gambetta* took over 650 sailors with her when she sank in April 1915. Fewer than 150 survived.

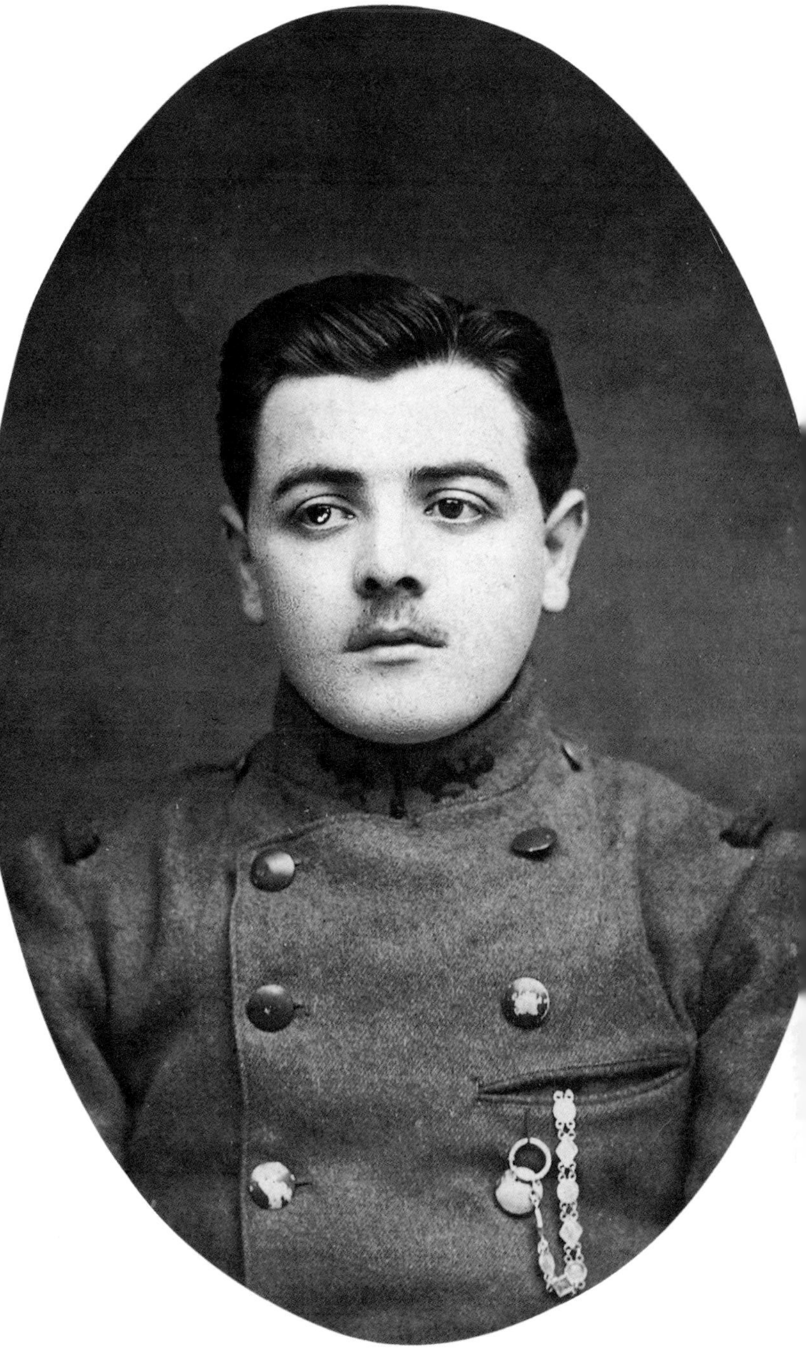

The marine infantryman in this studio photo wears a double-breasted wool tunic with painted metal buttons and two cloth anchors stitched to his collar.

These men from *infanterie de marine* are clad in various styles of caps and work fatigues. This photo is dated 14-12-15.

These three men in this studio photo are from the armored cruiser *Conde*, as the ribbons on their wool caps with pompoms indicate. Constructed in Lorient, this *Gloire* class armored cruiser saw service in the Atlantic squadron during the First World War.

These two marine infantrymen are clad in white cotton uniforms and wool pompom caps.

The sailor in this studio wears a dark wool uniform and cap with pompom. The word *"Compagne"* is written on the ribbon on his cap.

The NCO is this studio photo wears a wool kepi and summer weight cotton tunic and trousers. The reverse of this photo indicates it was taken in Saigon.

The colonial infantryman, or *infanterie coloniale*, in this studio photo wears a dark uniform over his striped *chemise* (shirt), and a dark wool cap with red pompom.

The sailor in this studio photo wears a dark wool uniform over his striped *chemise*, and a cotton cap with pompom.

These men wear cotton fatigues and caps with pompoms. The man seated on the right, holding his pith helmet, wears a summer weight cotton tunic and trousers. *"Farfadet"* is a class of submarines

The seven men wearing dark wool uniforms in this studio photo are from the destroyer *Poignard*, as indicated by the ribbon on those wearing caps with pompoms.

Chapter Nine

Foreign Legion/ Légion Etrangère

Many of the Legionnaires in this group photo are armed with 8mm Lebel caliber Lebel Model 1886/93 rifles and wear a white kepi often referred to as a *kepi blanc*.

The soldiers in this group photo pause for a photo while resting and enjoying drinks from their canteens, or *bidons*.

This mustached Legionnaire poses for a photo outside his tent wearing a khaki tunic with trousers. His khaki cloth covered pith helmet with leather chinstrap rests on the table to his left.

The two soldiers in this studio photo wear khaki tunics and trousers. The soldier on the left wears a khaki cloth covered pith helmet with leather chinstrap.

The three legionnaires in this prewar vintage photo pose while enjoying a drink.

This Legionnaire wears a white kepi, or *kepi blanc*, and a horizon blue wool tunic, which he has belted with a two pronged leather belt.

This 1917 vintage photo displays a variety of tunics and headdresses.

A pre to early war vintage photo of Legionnaires wearing white kepis and field shirts.

This group of decorated Legionnaires pose for a photo while standing at attention.

This group of soldiers pause for a photo wearing their white kepis and work fatigues.

Six of the seven Legionnaires in this studio photo wear white cotton uniforms and pith helmets. The Legionnaire on the left wears a khaki tunic with a white pith helmet. For the most part, such attire as seen here was worn by those serving in the tropical and desert regions of the Empire.

This group of Legionnaires clad in khaki uniforms and pith helmets proudly pose for a photo in the field.

Chapter Ten

Zouaves

The mustached Zouave in this studio photo wears a *shama*, or jacket, made of blue wool and embellished with madder red wool designs. Underneath his *shama* is a vest known as the *sédria*, which also was dark blue wool with madder red wool designs. He has a metal number "3" and crescent moon insignia fastened to his cylindrical shaped red wool cap, known as a *chéchia*.

The Zouave in this studio photo wears a cylindrical shaped red wool cap known as a *chéchia*. He wears a dark wool vest known as a *sédria* underneath his jacket, or *shama*. In addition, he wears fitted trousers instead of the baggy *sarouel*.

This Zouave wears *sarouel*, which are baggy trousers made of red wool with a slit located near the front known as a "*Lamoriciére*." This slit allowed water to be drained after having waded through a stream or lake. He has a metal number "3" and crescent moon insignia fastened to his cylindrical shaped red wool cap, known as a *chéchia*.

The mustached Zouave in this studio photo wears a *shama* made of blue wool and embellished with madder red wool designs. Underneath his *shama* is a vest known as the *sédria*, which also was dark blue wool with madder red wool designs. In addition, he wears *sarouel*, which are baggy trousers made of red wool with a slit located near the front known as a "*Lamoriciére*." This slit allowed water to be drained after having waded through a stream or lake.

This Zouave, wearing a *chéchia*, has been awarded the *Croix de Guerre*, which he has pinned to his double breast pocketed wool tunic. He has his trousers tucked into a privately purchased pair of leather boots.

The soldier in this 1916 vintage studio portrait wears a *chéchia* and a horizon blue wool tunic and trousers with puttees and ankle boots.

The Zouave in this studio photo wears a cylindrical shaped red wool cap known as a *chéchia*, and an overcoat made of coarse wool with his unit numbers stitched to his collar.

The Zouave in this studio photo wears a *chéchia* with a crescent moon insignia. His unit numbers are made of metal and fastened to the collar of his coarse wool tunic.

A late war vintage studio photo of a decorated Zouave wearing a dark wool tunic with rank distinctions stitched on the sleeves and cylindrical shaped red wool cap known as a *chéchia*.

Three of the four Zouaves in this late war vintage studio photo wear khaki tunics and trousers with unit numbers stitched to their collars. The Zouave standing on the left wears a *shama* (jacket) that was made of blue wool and embellished with madder red wool designs.

A mustached Zouave in a coarse wool overcoat and tunic pauses for a photo near an outpost. His *chéchia* bears no insignia.

The mustached Zouave in this late war vintage studio photo wears a coarse wool tunic with double breast and side pockets. He wears a cylindrical shaped red wool cap known as a *chéchia* bearing no insignia.

A pre to early war vintage photo of Zouaves, many of whom wear *chéchia*, *shama*, and *sarouel*.

The Zouaves in this late war vintage photo wear various styles of tunics, and a red wool cylindrical shaped cap known as a *chéchia*.

With the exception of the mustached NCO standing in the rear with his arms crossed, each Zouave wears a *chéchia*, *shama*, and *sarouel*.

North Africa, 1905.

The eight Zouaves in this late war vintage studio photo wear overcoats made of coarse wool with unit numbers stitched on the collars. Each wears a red wool cylindrical shaped cap known as a *chéchia*.

This photo was taken at a *Kriegsgefangenlager*, or Prisoner of War Camp, in Würtemberg, Germany, 1915.

The group of Zouaves in this late war vintage photo are clad in work fatigues. Many wear a red wool cylindrical shaped cap known as a *chéchia*.

Zouaves and civilians pose for a late war vintage group photo. The Zouaves are clad in wool tunics, with the unit numbers stitched to their collars. Each wears a red wool cylindrical shaped cap known as a *chéchia*.

A late war vintage photo of Zouaves and metropolitan troops.

Each Zouave in this pre to early war vintage photo wears a *chéchia* and a pair of baggy trousers. Some are holding their regulation drinking cup, or *quart réglementaire*. The Zouave seated center-right holds an iron shoe form and cobbler hammer.

Zouaves and metropolitan troops pause from their kitchen duties to pose for a photo.

This group of Zouaves pause for a photo wearing their wool tunics, with unit numbers stitched to their collars and field shirts. Each wears a red wool cylindrical shaped cap known as a *chéchia*.

A pre to early war vintage photo of Zouaves, many of whom wear *chéchia*, *shama*, and *sarouel*.

North Africa, "*Viva la Classe 17.*"

The mustached Zouave in this late war vintage studio photo wears a privately tailored tunic based on the Model 1915, and a red wool cylindrical shaped cap known as a *chéchia*.

The two Zouaves in this late war vintage studio photo wear privately tailored tunics based on the Model 1915, with unit numbers and a crescent moon motif stitched to their collars. The Zouave on the right wears a red wool cylindrical shaped cap known as a *chéchia* with a metal number "1" and crescent moon insignia.

Chapter Eleven

Tirailleurs

A wounded *tirailleur* poses for a photo taken in a *Kriegsgefangenlager* (POW camp).

This *tirailleur* has a marksman patch stitched to his left sleeve, and is armed with a Lebel bayonet.

Tunisian indigenous infantryman, or *Tirailleur Tunisien*.

A decorated *tirailleur* wearing a wool cylindrical cap poses for a photo with soldiers from other branches of service in the French armed forces. February 18, 1916.

A group of indigenous Moroccan military bandsmen.

A group of indigenous Moroccan infantrymen, or *Tirailleurs Marocain.*

A highly decorated Moroccan infantryman, or *Tirailleur Marocain.*

This is a patriotic photo postcard depicting Annamese nobles serving in a regiment of *tirailleurs* during the Great War.

Annamese soldiers ready to fight for the French armed forces in Salonica. This is a photograph from Underwood and Underwood, N.Y.

Chapter Twelve

POWs and Comrades in Arms

This unique photo shows a mustached French NCO from the 135 *Régiment* with a prisoner of war identification badge fastened to his dark colored wool *kepi*. The soldier on the left wears a wool *Feldkappe* (field cap) and *mantel* (overcoat) worn by soldiers in the *k.u.k*, or royal and imperial Austro-Hungarian armed forces. The description on the back of this photo, dated March 1, 1917, is written in German.

French and Imperial Russian soldiers pose for a 1916 vintage group photo clad in *kepis*, *furashki* (field caps), and *shineli* (overcoats).

At a *Kriegsgefangenlager* (Prisoner of War Camp) in Friedrichsfeld during September 1916, a group of French and Imperial Russian POWs pose for a photo wearing *kepis*, and *furashki* (field caps).

A group of POWs pose for a 1915 vintage photo postcard that is ink stamped on the reverse side "*Kriegsgefangenensendung*" and "*Geprüft*."

A group of French and Imperial Russian POWs/actors pose for a photo after having performed a play. April 22, 1915.

The mustached *poilu* seated in this photo is from the 72e *Régiment*, as the cloth numbers stitched to the collar of his horizon blue wool tunic indicate. His prisoner of war identification numbers are stitched above his left breast pocket.

The mustached *poilu* in this studio photo is from the 367 *Régiment*, as the metal numbers fastened to his collar indicate. His prisoner of war identification numbers are stitched to the button flap of his wool tunic. "*Souvenir de Mannheim*" is written on the reverse side of this photo.

Two mustached *poilus* pose for a photo wearing wool kepis and tunics bearing prisoner of war identification markings. The *poilu* on the right wears an armlet on his left sleeve with the words "*Kriegsgefanger Soldat*."

The *poilu* in this studio photo taken in April 1918 has prisoner of war identification markings stitched to his privately tailored wool tunic.

This mustached *poilu* wears corduroy trousers and a coarse wool tunic with prisoner of war identification markings stitched to his left breast pocket.

This *poilu* wears a horizon blue wool *kepi* with metal regiment numbers, and a tunic with a prisoner of war identification disk fastened above the right breast pocket.

Some of the first prisoners of war pose for a group photo clad in wool *kepis* and overcoats.

Seven mustached prisoners of war pose for a photo with their Imperial German captor wearing various styles of tunics.

This mustached *poilu* has a prisoner of war identification plaque fastened on his overcoat between the buttons.

This mustached *poilu* has prisoner of war identification plaques fastened on his dark wool *kepi* and tunic.

This mustached *poilu* has a prisoner of war identification disk fastened to his horizon blue wool tunic. Königsbrück, September 4, 1916.

Poilus and Imperial German soldiers pose for a photo outside of a wood outpost near the front.

Chapter Thirteen

Chasseurs, Tartes, and Berets

The bearded chasseur in this studio photo wears a dark colored wool *tarte*, and has two service chevrons stitched to the left sleeve of his overcoat. He has a Model 1892 *musette*, or general purpose bag, flung over his right shoulder, and a Model 1877 *bidon* (canteen) with regulation drinking cup over his left.

This *chasseur alpin* wears a dark blue wool *tarte* with hunting horn motif, and is armed with a 8mm Lebel caliber Lebel 1886/93 rifle.

The *poilu* in this studio photo wears a dark colored wool beret and a Model 1915 horizon blue wool tunic. He has regimental numbers stitched to his collar, and a machine gun aimer patch stitched to his left sleeve. His identification bracelet on his right wrist is visible, as well.

This mustached *chasseur* wears a dark wool *tarte* and privately tailored tunic with corduroy trousers.

Three mustached *poilus* clad in dark wool berets and Model 1915 horizon blue wool tunics. The *poilu* on the right carries a gasmask in his rectangular shaped metal canister.

This second lieutenant wears a horizon blue wool beret and overcoat. The reverse side of this photo is dated 3-2-16.

The *chasseur* in this studio photo wears a dark blue *tarte* and privately tailored tunic. "*Campagne 1914-15-1916*" is written on the reverse side of this photo.

Three mustached buglers pose for a photo wearing dark colored wool berets and horizon blue wool tunics.

The *chasseur* in this 1916 vintage studio photo wears a dark blue wool *tarte* with hunting horn motif and a privately tailored tunic with corduroy trousers.

This *chasseur* wears a wool *tarte* with a hunting horn motif. He has hunting horn motifs stitched to the collar of his tunic as well.

The two medics in this studio photo wear wool berets and Model 1915 horizon blue wool tunics.

The *poilu* in this 1917 vintage studio photo is from the 114 Régiment, and his beret, overcoat, and Model 1915 tunic are made of horizon blue wool.

The *chasseur* seated in this studio photo wears a dark blue wool *tarte* and a horizon blue wool tunic with trousers.

These two *chasseurs* wear dark blue wool *tartes* and horizon blue Model 1915 tunics.

The chasseur in this 1915 vintage studio photo wears a dark blue wool *tarte* with hunting horn motif and overcoat.

This lieutenant from 117 Régiment wears a beret, overcoat, and Model 1915 tunic made of horizon blue wool.

Ten *poilus* clad in berets, tent hats, work fatigues, and tunics.

A group of *chasseurs alpin* clad in dark blue *tartes* and tunics. A *chasseur* referred to his uniform as an outfit, or *tenue*. "*Souvenir de la Campagne de 1914-1915*" is written on the reverse side of this photo.

Chasseurs alpin pose for a photo on the side of a hill wearing dark blue wool *tartes*.

A group of *poilus* clad in dark colored wool berets, tunics, and well used cotton work fatigues.

Chasseurs, Zouaves, and metropolitan troops, 1916.

This group of *chasseurs* wear dark blue wool *tartes* and are armed with 8mm Lebel caliber Model 1916 Berthier rifles.

A group of *chasseurs* pose for a photo clad in dark blue wool *tartes* and cotton fatigues, as well as dark blue and horizon blue tunics.

A group of *chasseurs* wearing dark blue wool *tartes* and armed with 8mm Lebel caliber Model 1916 Berthier rifles, as well as Chauchat light machineguns.

This group of *chasseurs* wear dark blue wool *tartes* and horizon blue Model 1915 tunics.

Colonial machinegunners clad in dark blue wool berets and horizon blue wool tunics.

This group of *poilus* in this 1917 vintage photo wear wool berets, kepis, and Model 1915 horizon blue tunics.

Twenty-seven *chasseurs* pose proudly for a photo wearing dark blue wool *tartes* and tunics. A *chasseur* referred to his uniform as an outfit, or *tenue*.

This group of *chasseurs* wears dark blue wool *tartes* and horizon blue overcoats. The mustached officer seated front row center has chosen to wear a *kepi*.

Chapter Fourteen

Cuirassiers

The cuirassier in this pre to early vintage studio portrait has placed his plumed helmet on a pedestal. His cuirass hides the regimental numbers on the collar of this wool tunic.

A pre to early war cuirassier in full battle dress.

The mustached cuirassier in this pre to early war vintage studio photo proudly wears his plumed helmet and clutches his saber.

A group of pre to early war cuirassiers poses for a photo outside of the horse stables.

A group of pre to early war cuirassiers on parade.

A pre to early war cuirassier in full battle dress.

Chapter Fifteen

Mounted Troops

The three *chasseurs à cheval* from the 17e *Régiment* in this pre to early war vintage studio photo wear plumed shakos.

This mustached mounted artillerist rests his hands on his saber wearing wool tunic with braids, brass buttons, and gold-stitched rank chevrons on his sleeves.

Studio portraits such as this one were popular with the troops and boosted morale, as well as being humorous.

This mustached hussar wearing a wool kepi and tunic with braids poses proudly for a photo with his horse.

The mustached hussar clutching his saber in this pre to early war vintage studio photo wears a high collared wool tunic with braids.

A pre to early war photo of *chasseurs à cheval*. Those wearing shakos have removed their plumes, revealing their insignia.

Seven comrades from the 2 Régiment wearing dark colored wool *calottes* and tunics with braids.

This *chasseur à cheval*, with his plumed shako resting atop a pedestal, is from the 8 *Régiment*, as the numbers on the collar of his wool tunic with braids indicate.

This mustached hussar wearing a wool kepi and tunic with braids poses proudly for a photo with his horse in the field.

Seven *chasseurs à cheval* pose for a photo wearing wool kepis and tunics with braids, offering a look of early war barracks life.

Ten *chasseurs à cheval* pose for a photo wearing wool *calottes* and tunics with braids. Two have sapper insignia, and one a marksmen distinction stitched to their left sleeves.

Eight mounted artillerists pose for a photo outside their tents.

A group of mounted artillerists wearing dark colored wool kepis pose for a photo outside of their straw covered outpost.

Eighteen *chasseurs à cheval* pose proudly for this pre to early war vintage photo. The mustached *chasseur à cheval* seated on the ground wearing a kepi has sapper insignia stitched to the sleeves of his wool tunic with braids.

A group photo of officers and NCOs from mounted regiments wearing a variety of wool kepis and tunics.

Chasseurs à cheval wearing deplumed shakos and tunics with braids riding to the front.

Nine officers and NCOs from mounted regiments wearing a variety of wool kepis and tunics pose for a photo standing on a dirt road in a town near the Front.

Thirty-six *chasseurs à cheval* pose for a photo wearing first model forage caps, kepis, work fatigues, wool tunics with braids, and barracks clogs.

Two mounted artillerists pose for a photo outside their tent near the Front.

Twenty-five *chasseurs d'Afrique* pose for a pre to early war vintage photo wearing the first model forage cap, or *calotte premier type*.

Twenty-one *chasseurs à cheval* pose for a pre to early war vintage photo wearing forage caps, kepis, work fatigues, wool tunics with braids, and barracks clogs.

Eight mounted artillerists pose for a photo next to their 80mm caliber Model 1877 De Bange cannon.

Six mounted artillerists wearing the first model forage cap (*calotte premier type*) pause for a photo while enjoying a drink.

Chapter Sixteen

Dragoons

Twenty-one dragoons clad in dark wool tunics and plumed helmets pose with their 8mm caliber, French manufactured Model 1905 Puteaux, or *modele 1905 mitrailleuse Puteaux*, in this pre to early war vintage photo.

This is a commercially produced photo postcard depicting six dragoons manning an 8mm caliber, French manufactured Model 1905 Puteaux, or *modele 1905 mitrailleuse Puteaux*.

Twelve dragoons pose for a photo at the gate of their barracks wearing wool tunics, plumed helmets, fatigues, forage caps, and a kepi. The painted letters "*RF*" on the round plaque stand for *République Française*.

A mounted dragoon in full battledress. He has camouflaged his shiny helmet with a cloth cover.

The mustached dragoon in this pre to early war vintage studio photo has his plumed helmet resting on a pedestal. He is from the 12e *Régiment*, as the numbers on his collar indicate, and he has a marksmen distinction stitched to his left sleeve.

This mustached dragoon, with his hands resting on his saber in this pre to early war studio photo, wears a plumed helmet and a dark wool tunic.

These dragoons display the saddles and other equestrian gear used before and during the First World War.

A pre to early war dragoon.

Chapter Seventeen

Armor/Tanks

Two crewmen wearing berets with *Artillerie Spéciale* insignia and leather jackets pose proudly for a photo with their Renault F.T. 17 "*char canon*." Holding a maximum of two crewmen, a Renault F.T. 17 "*char canon*" weighed over six tons, and was armed with a 37mm caliber cannon.

Crewmen and mechanics wearing berets and fatigues pose for a photo with their Renault F.T. 17 "*char canon*" and "*char mitrailleur*." The "*char mitrailleur*" was armed with a French manufactured Hotchkiss 8mm caliber machinegun, or *la mitrailleuse Hotchkiss* (front), whereas the "*char canon*" was armed with a 37mm caliber cannon (rear). Both weighed over six tons and could reach speeds up to 8 kilometers per hour.

A Renault F.T. 17 "*char mitrailleur*" trying to make it up a hill. The "*char mitrailleur*" was armed with a French manufactured Hotchkiss 8mm caliber machinegun, or *la mitrailleuse Hotchkiss*.

Three children pose for a photo standing on the tracks and holding the 37mm caliber cannon of a Renault F.T. 17 "*char canon*" on display in Paris. This photo offers a view of the rear hatch.

A fabulous action photo showing a Renault F.T. 17 "*char canon*" supporting advancing allied infantry across no man's land as a BE 2c flies overhead.

This stunning action photo shows two BE 2cs flying over advancing allied infantry supported by a Renault F.T. 17 "*char canon*."

An abandoned Schneider M.16. This tank weighed over thirteen tons, and could hold up to seven crewmen. The armament of the tank consisted of a 75mm caliber cannon plus 8mm caliber machineguns.

Advancing camouflaged Schneider M.16 tanks.

A camouflaged 23 ton St. Chamond M.16 rolling into action armed with a 75mm caliber cannon and 8mm caliber machineguns. The St. Chamond M.16 could accommodate up to nine crewmen.

Five *poilus* standing next to an armored car armed with a light cannon and a 8mm caliber machinegun.

A Model 1913 De Dion Bouton automobile with 75mm cannon, or *l'auto canon de 75 De Dion Bouton modéle 1913*. This Model 1913 De Dion Bouton was used as an anti-aircraft, or as an infantry support vehicle. Rocquencourt April 3, 1918.

An armored car on a dirt road in St. Julian, near Cambrai.

The inscription on the side of this destroyed tank reads "Erledigte von der bayerische Nahkampfbatterie 16 IV 17," or " Taken care of or, Knocked-out by the Bavarian Close Combat Battery on April 16, 1917."

A group of tank crewmen wearing dark wool berets with *Artillerie Spéciale* insignia, Model 1915 horizon blue wool tunic, and fatigues.

Many a Renault F.T. 17 "*char canon*," as well as "*char mitrailleur*" saw service in other countries during the years following the Great War.

The crewman in this studio photo wears a dark wool beret with *Artillerie Spéciale* insignia fastened to the front, and a privately tailored horizon blue wool tunic with an *Artillerie Spéciale* patch stitched to his left sleeve.

Chapter Eighteen

Pre to Early War

The two mustached *poilus* in this pre to early war vintage studio photo are from the 66 *Régiment*, as the numbers on the collars of their dark blue wool tunics indicate. The hooks on their bayonets would most likely have been removed as the war progressed, because of the tendency to catch on barbed wire while bayoneting.

The two *poilus* in this pre to early war studio photo are from the 153 *Régiment*, as the numbers on the their wool kepis and overcoat collars indicate. Both wear an earlier model of belt with a smooth brass buckle.

A 1914 vintage studio photo of a *poilu* with a *musette*, or general purpose bag, flung over his shoulder. He wears an early model dark blue wool kepi and overcoat. The roll on his right shoulder kept his rifle from slipping off.

Five *poilus* wearing early model kepis and tunics pause from their card playing and drinking from their regulation drinking cups for a photo.

A pre to early war studio photo of a *poilu* from the 27 *Régiment* wearing a dark colored wool tunic with a marksmen patch stitched to his left sleeve.

The two *poilus* in this pre to early war vintage photo are wearing dark blue wool kepis with cloaks that attach to their overcoats.

Two *poilus* from the 33 *Régiment* clad in dark blue wool kepis and nine button waistcoats, which they have belted with two pronged leather belts. This style of waistcoat was known as a *ras le cul*.

Two *poilus* from the 17 Régiment clad in dark blue wool kepis and nine button waistcoats. This style of waistcoat was known as a *ras le cul*.

This *poilu* poses proudly for a photo wearing an early model wool kepi and double breasted overcoat.

These two *poilus* wear dark blue wool kepis with nine button waistcoats (*ras le cul*), and are armed with holstered revolvers.

Thirteen poilus clad in dark blue wool kepis and nine button waistcoats pose for a photo next to their wagons.

Ten *poilus* dressed in pre to early war vintage dark blue wool uniforms. The numbers "*25*" on their kepis and collars of their tunics indicate their unit.

This group of *poilus* camped in a wood pose for a photo wearing dark blue wool kepis, first model tent hats, nine button waistcoats, white cotton fatigues, and wool overcoats.

The *poilu* seated on the right, as well as the one standing behind the woman are from the 59e *Régiment*, as the numbers on their dark colored wool kepis and collars of their tunics indicate. The other *poilu* wearing a leather jacket is in the medical corps, as the gold-stitched insignia on his collar reveals.

The home guardsmen in this photo wear early model dark wool kepis and tunics, as well as tunics made of corduroy or civilian dress. Four of these home guardsmen are armed with 8mm Lebel caliber Gras 1874/80/14 bolt-action rifles.

Three *poilus* from mounted units clad in early model dark wool kepis and tunics.

The ten *poilus* in this studio portrait are from the 161 *Régiment*, as the numbers on their dark colored wool kepis and collars of their overcoats indicate. *Poilus* often wrote on their dark colored wool tunics with chalk, as seen here in this photo.

This group of *poilus* wearing dark blue wool kepis, first model tent hats, nine button waistcoats, and wool overcoats pauses for a photo while preparing a meal using issued mess equipment. Writing on their dark wool uniforms with chalk was popular with *poilus*.

Eight poilus from the 142e *Régiment*. Four have marksmen distinctions stitched to the sleeves of their nine button dark blue wool waistcoats. This style of waistcoat was known as a *ras le cul*.

Six soldiers in full battledress pose for a photo before heading to the front. Each is armed with a 8mm Lebel caliber Lebel 1886/93 bolt-action rifle.

The *poilu* standing with his arms at his side wears a dark blue wool kepi and a nine button waistcoat known as a *ras le cul*. The other two *poilus* wear dark blue wool kepis and overcoats, and are armed with 8mm Lebel caliber Lebel 1886/93 bolt-action rifles.

Fifteen *poilus* clad in dark wool kepis and overcoats pose for a photo with their regulation mess equipment.

A group of *poilus* wearing dark wool kepis and tunics pose for a photo at the edge of a wood. Several are armed with 8mm Lebel caliber Lebel 1886/93 bolt-action rifles.

Some of the first POWs pose for a commemorative photo.

A group of *poilus* armed with 8mm Lebel 1886/93 bolt-action rifles.

A group of *poilus* clad in dark blue wool kepis and overcoats resting after a march. This photo displays how mess equipment was transported.

Thirteen *poilus* from the 71e *Régiment* armed with 8mm Lebel caliber Lebel 1886/93 bolt-action rifles pose for a photo at edge of a wood.

A group of *poilus* from the 89e *Régiment* pose for a photo wearing dark blue kepis and uniforms.

This group of *poilus* wears their rolled wool blankets across their chests, and are armed with 8mm Lebel caliber Berthier carbines.

A pre to early war vintage photo of dragoons from the 10e *Régiment*.

A cluster of *poilus* in a camp near the front. Several are armed with 8mm Lebel caliber Lebel 1886/93 bolt-action rifles.

Soldiers from various branches of the armed forces pose for a commemorative photo.

The eight *poilus* in this pre to early war vintage studio photo have cloth covers over their dark blue wool kepis, and are armed with 8mm Lebel 1886/93 bolt-action rifles.

Thirty-eight *poilus* pose for a pre to early war vintage photo wearing dark blue wool kepis, nine button waistcoats, first model forage caps, and work fatigues.

A group of *poilus* in 1915 wearing dark blue wool kepis with cotton covers.

This group of *poilus*, armed with 8mm Lebel caliber Lebel 1886/93 bolt-action rifles, is from the 46e *Régiment*, as the numbers on their kepis indicate.

A group of *poilus* clad in dark blue wool kepis and overcoats pose for a photo on a dirt road. This photo displays how mess equipment is carried on their backpack.

Four *poilus* resting outside their tent in a wooded area.

This group of *poilus* pauses from their meal for a photo, showing various types of mess equipment.

Nineteen *poilus* from the 276e *Régiment* clad in dark blue wool overcoats and kepis.

A group of *poilus* clad in various styles of overcoats, tunics, and fatigues. Many are armed with 8mm Lebel 1886/93 bolt-action rifles.

Nineteen *poilus* in dark blue wool kepis and armed with 8mm Lebel 1886/93 bolt-action rifles.

Thirteen *poilus* pose for a pre to early war vintage photo dressed in wool kepis, first model forage caps, nine button waistcoats, and cotton fatigues. *Poilus* often wrote on their wool tunics and headdresses with chalk.

Three poilus dressed in dark blue wool nine button waistcoats and kepis. The number "*45*" on their waistcoats and kepis indicates their unit. This style of waistcoat is known as a *ras-le-cul*.

Twelve *poilus* pose for a photo with their bayonets fixed and fingers near the triggers of their 8mm Lebel 1886/93 bolt-action rifles. The *poilu* on the right poses dressed in a *ras-le-cul* and *calotte*.

Eleven *poilus* dressed in dark blue wool kepis and tunics. The number "94" on their kepis and the collars of their tunics indicate their unit. The three *poilus* seated in the center on the bench have marksmen distinctions stitched to their left sleeves.

Nine *poilus* wearing dark blue wool kepis and nine button waistcoats. The number "75" on their kepis and the collars of their tunics indicate their unit. This style of waistcoat is referred to as a *ras-le-cul*.

A group of *poilus* clad in dark blue wool kepis, tunics, overcoats, and cotton fatigues pose for a photo alongside a dirt road.

Eight poilus in a 1914 vintage photo dressed in cotton work fatigues, wool kepis, and first model forage caps. The poilu seated on the bench to the right holds an 8mm Lebel 1886/93 bolt-action rifle in his right hand.

Zouaves and *chasseurs* pose for a commemorative photo.

Poilus in full battledress ready for action.

A pre to early war group of *poilus*.

The *poilus* in this group photo are dressed in cotton fatigues, and are armed with 8mm Lebel 1886/93 bolt-action rifles.

A group of mounted artillerists dressed in pre to early war vintage uniforms, with their *musettes* (general purpose bags) and *quart réglementaire* (regulation drinking cups).

Eight *poilus* dressed in cotton work fatigues, and three dressed in nine button wool waistcoats. This style of waistcoat was referred to as a *ras le cul*.

This group of *poilus* is in full battledress, and are armed with 8mm Lebel 1886/93 bolt-action rifles.

Twelve *poilus* dressed in cotton fatigues and nine button wool waistcoats pose for a photo inside their barracks.

Ten *poilus* dressed in wool kepis and overcoats, as well as cotton fatigues. *Poilus* often wrote on their uniforms in chalk.

Chapter Nineteen

Late to Post War

Renault F.T. 17 tanks roll through the *l'Arc de Triomphe*. July 14, 1919.

Victorious French armed forces parading by cheering crowds on the Champs d' Elssye.

A late to post war presentation ceremony.

Breguet 19 biplanes in flight.

This photo of a Breguet 19 biplane was taken in flight over fields in France.

Two Breguet 19 biplanes in flight.

Breguet 19 biplanes in flight.

Breguet 19 biplanes in flight

A Breuguet 19 after a crash landing.

A group of *poilus* clad in horizon blue wool overcoats, tunics, forage caps, and Model 1915 Adrian helmets.

Eight *poilus* dressed in horizon blue wool forage caps, tunics, and a kepi pose proudly with their 8mm caliber tripod mounted Hotchkiss machinegun and Berthier carbines.

A group of Legionaires pose proudly for a photo with a light caliber field cannon and cluster of hand grenades.

Chapter Twenty

Life on the Front and in the Trenches

This *poilu*, clad in a Model 1915 Adrian helmet and horizon blue wool tunic, prepares for an enemy advance with a grenade in his right hand. He has his gasmask in the rectangular metal canister hanging from his neck. His 8mm Lebel 1886/93 bolt-action rifle leans against the sandbag fortification near a trench periscope. 1916.

Three medics and two infantrymen pose for a photo by the firing holes of a sandbag fortification.

A medic in a dark colored wool tunic with horizon blue kepi, and an infantryman in a horizon blue overcoat with kepi pose for a photo in a lightly fortified trench.

This *poilu*, holding on to his bicycle, wears a Model 1915 horizon blue wool tunic and forage cap.

These three *poilus*, clad in full battledress, are armed with 8mm Lebel 1886/93 bolt-action rifles.

Two *poilus* preparing to launch a grenade from their lightly fortified position.

Poilus in Model 1915 Adrian helmets and horizon blue wool tunics stringing barbed wire over a communication trench.

A fabulous action shot of brave *poilus* firing a trench mortar from a forward position.

Poilus and Anzacs pose for a photo as comrades in arms in this 1917 vintage photo.

This group of *poilus* pause for a photo with their picks, shovels, and wheelbarrows before digging trenches.

Fifteen *poilus* clad in Model 1915 Adrian helmets, horizon blue tunics, forage caps, and kepis pose for a photo on the front, 1917.

Poilus strolling through a town ravaged by shellfire.

Poilus advancing through a forest in full battledress, armed with 8mm Lebel 1886/93 bolt-action rifles, pause for a photo.

Seven *poilus* from the 78e *Régiment* pose for a photo clad in full gear, and armed with 8mm Lebel 1886/93 bolt-action rifles. Six of the seven have cotton covers for their dark blue wool kepis.

Fourteen *poilus* dressed in fatigues and horizon blue wool tunics pause from eating their meal using regulation mess equipment.

Poilus in a camp near the front pose for a photo outside the tent. The *poilu* second from the right, wearing a dark blue wool kepi, has a marksmanship distinction stitched to the left sleeve of his *ras le cul*.

Poilus pause for a photo while standing guard over a stone bridge.

A group of *poilus* in cotton fatigues and dark blue wool kepis and tunics pause from eating their meal using regulation mess equipment.

Five *poilus* enjoying a drink at their outpost near the front. The *poilu* standing in the center has three service chevrons stitched to the left sleeve of his Model 1915 horizon blue wool tunic.

This group of *poilus*, dressed in dark blue wool kepis and overcoats, is from the 168 *Régiment*. Many are holding their regulation drinking cup. 1914.

Four *poilus* wearing Model 1915 horizon blue wool tunics pose for a photo in front of their outpost.

A group of *poilus* pose for a photo at their outpost.

A group of poilus clad in dark blue wool kepis, overcoats, and tunics pauses for a photo before continuing their march to the front.

A regimental priest wearing a Model 1915 Adrian helmet stares at his watch before the hour of destiny arrives.

Poilus wearing Model 1915 Adrian helmets march to the frontline through a communications trench protected by barbed wire.

Poilus with their canine friends in the trenches.

Poilus wearing Model 1915 horizon blue wool tunics and forage caps pose for a photo at a frozen section of the Maginot line.

Poilus wearing dark blue wool kepis and tunics pose for a photo with their caissons, wagons, and horses in the background.

A group of *poilus* wearing kepis and horizon blue wool overcoats.

This group of *poilus* clad in Model 1915 horizon blue wool tunics, overcoats, and forage caps is from the 172e *Régiment*.

Poilus clad in dark blue wool kepis and overcoats pause for a photo before continuing on their march.

Eight *poilus* in dark blue wool kepis and overcoats pause for a photo while enjoying a drink in a town near the front.

Poilus posing for a photo in a railroad yard, 1915.

A group of *poilus* wearing dark blue wool kepis, tunics, and cotton fatigues pose for a photo with their picks and shovels. This photo was taken near an aerodrome, as an airplane and hangars are visible in the background.

Five *poilus* wearing early war tunics and headdresses pose for a photo with a bicycle.

A group of *poilus* eagerly watch and listen while their officers study maps and reports.

The *poilu* on the right wears a dark blue wool kepi with a corduroy tunic and trousers. The other two *poilus* wear dark blue wool kepis and nine button waistcoats. This style of waistcoat is known as a *ras le cul*.

Four *poilus* wearing dark blue wool tunics with white trousers relaxing outside their tent.

A company of *poilus* pose for a photo at the edge of a forest.

This group of *poilus* clad in dark blue wool kepis, overcoats, and tunics pose for a photo on a dirt road in a wooded area.

A pre to early war vintage photo of a group of *poilus* in dark blue wool kepis, overcoats, and tunics.

A group of *poilus* clad in dark blue wool kepis, overcoats, and tunics pose for a photo with their rifles and wagons in the background.

In trenches on the western front.

Three *poilus* preparing to fire from their dugout on the western front.

French *chasseurs* and United States soldiers (Dough boys) digging in on the western front.

Poilus pose for a photo at a destroyed fortification on the western front.

Poilus studying maps and reports at an outpost on the western front.

Poilus en route to the frontlines.

Poilus awaiting orders for an attack.

Chapter Twenty-One

The Generals

French and other allied generals and officers conversing over a drink, 1917.

French generals riding victoriously through *l'Arc de Triomphe*.

Acknowledging the troops as they march by.

French pilots Fonck and Heurleaux with General Anthoine.

General Degoutte

General Mangin

General Fayolle

General Humbert

General Petain

General Foch

Color Gallery

Wool Zouave *shama* (waistcoat) with cotton lining and depot stamps.

Wool Zouave *sedria* (vest) with depot stamped cotton back.

Wool *chechia* with brass insignia.

Depot stamped madder red wool pants, or *les pantaloons garance*.

Depot stamped khaki *Marine d'Infanterie* tropical/summer weight tunic, or *Veste d'Infanterie de Marine*, with brass anchor buttons.

Wool *Dolman* with cotton lining.

Wool *chasseurs a' cheval* tunic with depot stamped cotton lining.

Wool tunic with brass buttons and depot stamped cotton lining for mounted artillerists.

Wool *Ras le Cul*, or waistcoat, with brass artillery buttons and depot stamped cotton lining.

Privately tailored wool tunic with brass artillery buttons and cotton lining. *Veste d' un Commandant (Chef de Groupe).*

Wool cloak/cape (*colet*) with brass artillery buttons and ink stamped cotton manufacturer's label.

Black wool kepi with brass artillery buttons and silk lining for a *Commandant (Chef de Groupe) d'artilleur*.

Kepi bleu Horizon Modele 1915 'un Capitaine d'Artillerie Model 1915. Horizon blue wool kepi for an artillery captain.

Calot d'Artilleur Premier Type, or First Model Forage Cap for Artillerists.

Calot d' Artilleur Forage Cap for Artillerists with red piping.

Calot d' Infanterie. Roughly cut wool infantry forage cap with depot stamped cotton sweatband.

Calot d' Infanterie. Wool infantry forage cap with dark blue piping and rank stripe.

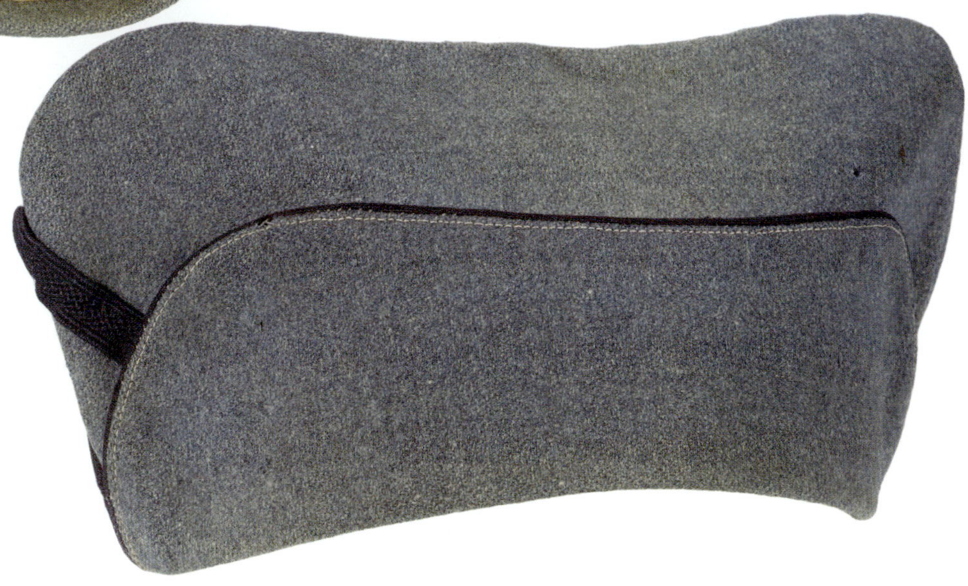

United States manufactured horizon blue wool forage cap with an embossed leather sweatband and bronze cap badge for supply train troops.

Dark blue wool navy cap with red pom-pom and piping for *Torpilleurs de Brest* (Torpedo Crews). Interior lining is waterproof.

Model 1915 Adrian steel helmet for infantry with a high gloss horizon blue paint finish. Liner and chin-strap are leather.

Brass visor plate for the Model 1915 Adrian steel helmet worn by veterans of the Great War.

Model 1915 Adrian steel helmet with both a horizon blue and mustard color matte paint finish for Marine Infantry troops. The leather liner has been removed, offering a detailed view of the interior construction.

Model 1915 Adrian steel helmet painted horizon blue with a matte finish for Engineers. Liner and chinstrap are leather.

Model 1915 Horizon blue wool tunic with depot stamped cotton lining for enlisted rank line infantry.

Ink stamps on the interior cotton lining of a Model 1915 Horizon blue wool tunic.

Forward and reverse side of an infantry button.

Model 1915 Horizon blue wool tunic. *Veste Modele 1915 Bleu Horizon*

Model 1915 Horizon blue wool tunic for a solider in the 39th Regiment.

Privately tailored Model 1915 Horizon blue wool tunic with brass artillery buttons.

Veste d' Aspirant Medecin Bleu Horizon - Horizon Blue Wool Tunic for a Medical Apirant (Candidate for Second Lieutenant).

Wool Insignia Patches

Row 1 Mechanic, Bicyclist , Mechanic
Row 2 Driver (Red), Signaler, Driver (Blue)

Row 3 Ski unit (Red), 19th Chassuers, Ski unit (Blue)
Row 4 Shoemaker/ Cobbler (Red), Electro-mechanic, Shoemaker/ Cobbler (Blue)

Privately made leather ankle boots with wood soles and metal hobnails.

Privately purchased lace-up leather boots. This style of boot was preferred by NCOs and officers. The left boot shows repair from damage, most likely caused by a barbwire entanglement.

Depot stamped canvas backpack with leather trim and fittings.

Forward and reverse view of a depot stamped *musette*.

Canteen (*Bidon*) with leather carrying strap and horizon blue wool cover. Attached to the canteen is a regulation drinking cup.

Medical Canteen, or *Bidon*, painted white with a leather carrying strap. The red letter "A" stands for "ambulance."

Tobacco Rations

Mess tin, or *Gamelle*.

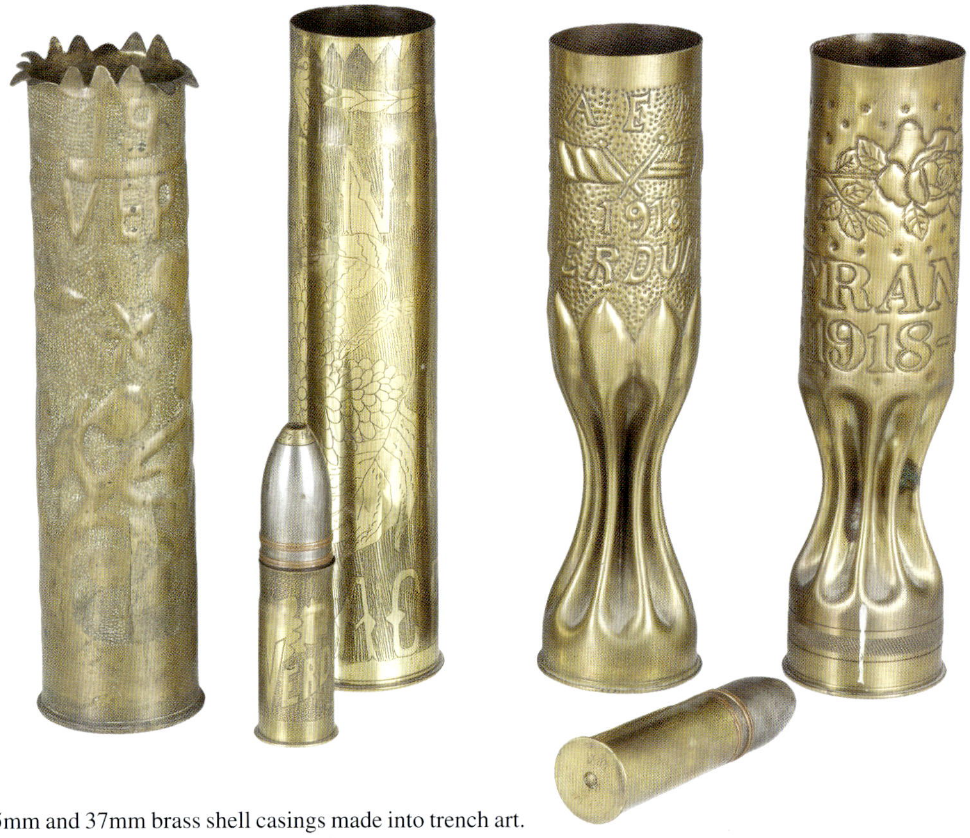

French manufactured 75mm and 37mm brass shell casings made into trench art.

Brass clinometer with leather carrier and 1918 manufacture date.

Forward and Reverse views of the *Croix de Guerre*, Medaille, Militaire, and a French manufactured victory medal.

French manufactured binoculars with leather carrying case.

This is a patriotic postcard depicting the Blessed Virgin Mary watching over a sleeping *poilu* and a dragoon. This text translates "For God and Country."

This is a patriotic postcard depicting Saint Joan of Arc guiding a *poilu*. The text translates " A vision of Saint Joan of Arc. The Cross of Joan of Arc dearest French soldier the final success is on you."

This is a patriotic postcard depicting an Italian Bersagliere and a French Zouave. The text translates " Reunited for the same ideal /cause."

This is a patriotic postcard depicting a conquered Hun or Imperial German soldier. The text translates "The citizens never forget the sacrifice for the country."

This is both a romantic and patriotic postcard depicting an aviator with flight insignia fastened to his beret and wreathed in flowers over an aerodrome.

Both a romantic and patriotic postcard depicting an aviator, this of his sweetheart with his biplane overhead. The text translates " Absent my love my heart beats for you night and day!"

A romantic and patriotic postcard depicting a dragoon in a plumed brass helmet. The text translates " An affectionate souvenir of..."

This patriotic postcard displays a *poilu*, a Belgian, and a British soldier united as brothers in arms on the Western Front, while the Cossacks ride above them to the Eastern Front. The text translates " United against the Barbarians."

POUR FAIRE UN POILU
Il faut avoir du poil dessus
Du poil aux yeux, du poil partout,
(Sauf dans la main) avoir surtout
Du poil...sous-entendu !!
Il faut avoir le cœur joyeux,
Lorsque ça pète et que ça crache,
Et des grelots à son panache,
Il en faut au moins deux !!
JK
2110
Il faut savoir tuer le cafard
Lorsque la perme se débine,
Et boire un bon coup de Pinard
A défaut.....d'un coup de chopine!
Il faut avoir l'esprit fertile,
Narguer le feu, l'eau et la boue:
Il faut savoir tomber debout......
Et ça c'est le plus difficile !

"To Be A *Poilu*!"

Glossary

L'Armée Français (Army, Cavalry and Artillery)

l'artillerie	Artillery (Field Cannons)
l' artillerie d'Afrique	North African Artillery
l'artillerie de forteresse	Fortress Artillery
l' artillerie spéciale	Tanks/ Armor
chasseur d'Afrique	African Cavalry
chasseur alpinsy	Alpine/Mountain troops
chasseur á cheval	Cavalry/Mounted troops
chasseur á pied	Foot soldiers
cuirassier	Cavalry (Breastplate)
dragons	Dragoons
escadron du train	Motor Transport
le genie	Engineers
le masque a gaz	Gasmask
la gamelle	Mess kit
la gendarmeri	Military Police/ Constable
hussards	Hussars
pontonniers	Pontoon bridge Construction
les sapeurs-pompiers	Fire Department
spahis	Indigenous Light Cavalry
tiraillеury	Sharpshooter/Indigenous troops
tirailleurs Algeriens	Indigenous Algerian Infantry
tirailleurs Annamites	Indigenous Annamese Infantry
tirailleurs Malgaches	Indigenous Madagascar Infantry
tirailleurs Marocains	Indigenous Moroccan Infantry
tirailleurs Senegalais	Indigenous Senegalese Infantry
tirailleurs Tunisiens	Indigenous Tunisian Infantry
zouaves	Zouaves

Aviation

un aéroplane	Airplane
un aeronaut	Dirigible
les ailerons	Ailerons
un avion	Airplane
un aviateur	Aviator
un avion de bombardement	Bomber/ Bombarding plane
un avion de chasse	Combat/Battle aircraft
un avion de reconnaissance	Reconnaissance / Reconnoitering plane
un avion de réglage de tir d' artillerie	Range registering plane
un biplan Biplane	
un canon contre-avion	Anti-aircraft gun
un dirigeable	Dirigible
une escadrille d' aéroplanes	Airplane squadron
le gonflement	Filling a balloon
un hangar	Hangar
une hélice	Propeller
huit cylindres	Eight Cylinder
hydro-avion	Seaplane
la locomotion aérienne	Flying
un monoplan	Monoplane
un motor	Motor
la navigation aérienne	Flying
un observateur	Observer
piquer	Dive
piquer du nez	Nose Dive
un section d'aérostiers	Balloon section
survoler	Fly over
la photgraphie aérienne	Aerial photography
un triplan	Tri-plane
un viseur	Bombsight

la Marine Française (Navy)

un amiral	Admiral
l'ancre	Anchor
le cabestan	Capstan
le capitaine de vaisseau	Captain
chef d'escadre	Commodore
le commis de vivres	Steward
contre-amiral	Rear Admiral
un débardeur, arrimeur	Stevedore
l'infanterie de Marine	Marines
maitre d'equipage	Boatswain
un matelot	Sailor
une torpille	Torpedo
un torpilleur sous-marin	Submarine
un vaisseau	Ship

Ranks

Maréchal de France	Marshal of France
Général de Division	Major General
Général de Brigade	Brigadier General
Colonel	Colonel
Lieutenant-Colonel	Lieutenant Colonel
Commandant	Major
Chef d'Escadron	Major (Artillery/Cavalry)
Capitaine	Captain
Lieutenant	First Lieutenant
Sous Lieutenant	Second Lieutenant
Adjudant	Adjutant
Aspirant	Candidate for Second Lieutenant
Maréchal des logis chef	Chief Sergeant
Maréchal des logis	Sergeant
Brigadier	Corporal
Premier Soldat	Private 1st class
Soldat de deuxiéme	Private

Commands

Descendez dans l'abricaverne.	Get down in the dugout.
En Marche!	Forward!
En avant!	Over the top!
Garde á vous!	Attention!
Nous sommes dans la lére vague d'assaut.	We are attacking in the first wave.
Repos!	Stand easy! At ease.
Voici le boyau d'accés.	Here is the access trench.
Peid 'a terre!	Dismount!

Equipment, weapons, and other military terms

une action d'éclat	Heroic Act
un alerte	Alarm
appareil respiratoire special	ARS17 Gasmask
l'artilleur	Artillerist
l'attaque	Attack
une automobile blindée	Armored Car
une baïonnette	Bayonet
le porte- baïonnette	Bayonet frog
une balle	Bullet
un bataillon	Battalion
une batery	Battery
une bataille	Battle
bidon	Canteen (Modele 1877)
une blessure	Wound
blindé	Armor plated
bleu horizon	Horizon blue
boulangerie de campagne	Field Bakery
bonnet de police	Forage Cap
un brassard	Armband / Armlet
Bretelles de Suspension	Leather Y- straps
Brevet	Patent (Stamped on most items)
Brodequins	Field Shoes/ Ankle Boots
Bottes	Boots
un calot	Forage cap
cantine médicale	Medical kit
un cannonier	Gunner
cartouchiéres	Ammo/Cartridge pouches
capote	Overcoat
une caserne	Armory (Infantry)
un casque	Helmet
ceinturon	Waist belt
le champ	Field
chéchia	Fez with a tassel
un clairon	Bugle
un collet	Cloak
un combat	Action
une compagnie	Company
un cordonnier	Shoemaker
un coup de fusil	Shot
le courage	Courage
couverture	Blanket (rolled)
la Croix de Genéve	Red Cross
la Croix de Guerre	The War Service Cross

Citations and distinctions on the ribbon

Bronze Star - Regiment
Silver Star- Division
Gold Star- Corps
Palm- Army

Crochets de Cuivre	Metal J-hooks
le drapeau	Flag
un éléve d'une école militaire	Cadet
une embuscade	Ambuscade /Ambush
un engagement	Action/Engagement
un épée	Sword
un escadron	Squadron
une escouade	Squad
l'étrier	Stirrup
l'étui-revolver	Holster
fils de fer barbelés	Barbed Wire
le flanc	Flank
une fortification	Fortification
fourrage	Fodder
un fusil	Rifle
une gourde	Canteen (Modele 1877)
gamelle	Mess kit
la garde	Guard
les pantalons garance	Red trousers
une grenade	Grenade
la guerre	War
un soldat de garde	Guardsman
une hache	Axe
jambiéres/molletiéres	Leggings
une jugulaire	Chinstrap
Légion Etrangére	Foreign Legion
les lunettes	Goggles
un magasin	Magazine
le manchon métallique	Metal jacket
manteau	Overcoat
le masques á gaz	Gasmasks
une marche en avant	Advance
le matériel d'atrillerie	Ordnance
une mine	Mine
une mitrailleuse	Machinegun
un mortier	Mortar
un musette	Breadbag
un obusier	Howitzer
une plaque d'identité	Indentity Disk/Dog tag
les pertes	Casualties
un poilu	A French Soldier (Literal translation-"The Hairy One" Latin=*pilus*=hair)
un quartier	Armory (Artillery/Cavalry)
quart réglementaire	drinking cup
une ration	Ration
rang, grade	Rank
ras-le-cul	Waistcoat/tunic
un revolver	Revolver
un sac de terre	Sandbag
sarouel	Baggy pants (Zouave)
une selle	Saddle
sédria	Vest (Zouave)
shama	Jacket (Zoave)
une tranchée	Trench
un tireur	Marksman
tué á l'ennemi	Killed in action
tunique	Tunic (Usually officer)
vareuse	Tunic
veste	Tunic

Further Reading

The Guns of August, Barbara Tuchman, The Macmillan Publishing Company, New York, 1962.

Militaria Magazine. A French language publication on military history.

French Aircraft of the First World War, Dr. James J. Davilla and Arthur M. Soltan, Fly Machines Press, Boulder, Colorado, 1997.

Great Battles of World War One, Anthony Livesey, The Macmillan Publishing Company, New York, 1989.

Paths of Glory; The French Army 1914-18, Anthony Clayton, Orion Publishing Group Limited, London, 2003.

Revue Historique des Armées. A French language publication on military history

The Price of Glory; Verdun 1916, Alister Horne, Penguin, New York, 1964.